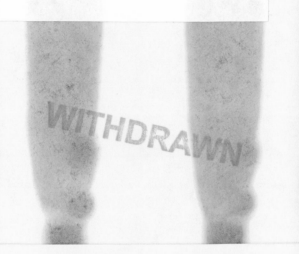

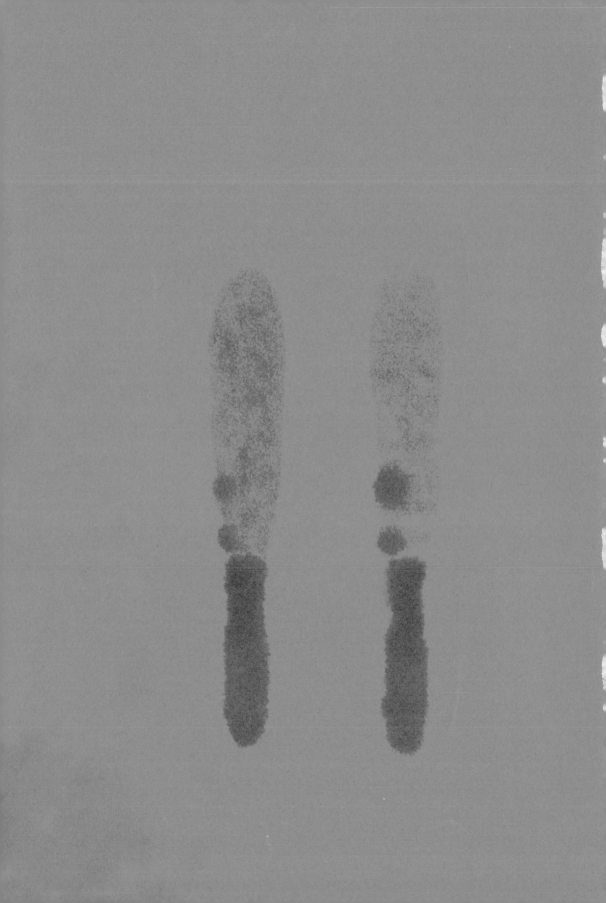

AUDI
QUATTRO

HIGH PERFORMANCE

·S·E·R·I·E·S·

AUDI QUATTRO

ALAN HENRY

ARCO PUBLISHING, INC.
NEW YORK

Published 1984 by Arco Publishing, Inc.
215 Park Avenue South, New York, NY 10003

Library of Congress Catalog Card Number: 83-73408

ISBN 0 668 06144 8

Design and Phototypesetting by Logos Design & Advertising,
Datchet, Berkshire, England.
Printed in Great Britain.

CONTENTS

INTRODUCTION

It is with great pleasure I accepted the invitation to write this introduction to a book about the Audi Quattro. Certainly, as rally fans will know, it is a car for which I have special feelings, since the Audi Quattro has played an important part in my career as a professional rally driver and the achievements I have gained in the sport.

I think there has been no other rally car to be so successful in such a short time and it stays at the front of competition with just a little development here and there.

Audi is still young in motorsport terms, but achieved so much with the Audi Quattro over just three seasons, including both the World Manufacturers and Drivers championships and winning most of the world's top events. For me that first world championship win by a woman, on the 1981 San Remo Rally, was very special but I don't feel that being a woman makes any difference. I am part of the Audi Sport team and absolutely no different to the other team members – Hannu Mikkola, Stig Blomqvist and Walter Rohrl.

The Audi Quattro has become so successful that it feels like there was never a time it wasn't around. You have to take a look at the records to remind yourself its unique four-wheel drive system is relatively new. It was only in 1981 the car was announced to the public and given its debut in rallying as well. I know Audi never envisaged producing more than about 400 for homologation and restricted sale at first, but now more than that many have been sold in Britain alone. Audi tells me their factory at Ingolstadt has built well over 6,500 versions of the Quattro for sale worldwide.

We in the rally team are pleased that our efforts to win for Audi have benefited customers on the road. Rallying is one of the toughest ways of proving a car and Audi has clearly demonstrated the value of its engineering approach in this way.

The Quattro four-wheel drive system provides fantastic traction and the car has well-developed handling. It was not surprising Audi decided to use rallying as the way of showing people how good it is. And then to extend that to other Audi models is fantastic.

I know the rally Quattro is a very special and expensive machine, but production models like the Audi 80 Quattro now bring this fantastic concept within the reach of more people. You don't need bad conditions to find out how good a Quattro is, they just make it so clear.

The reaction of other car manufacturers to the Audi system has shown how good it is. They are all trying to develop their own, yet the Audi remains ahead and has plans to stay that way.

Succeeding in world championship and national rallies has also given Audi a new image, taking it away from the days when an Audi was the car only for old people. Today as we travel from one event to the next, it is easy to see Audi drivers of all ages. I am not so old myself and I really do enjoy driving Audi cars, particularly my Quattro. I have never got stuck in bad weather anywhere and that is always a worry when you have to make important meetings or catch flights to rallies.

I am sure you will find Alan Henry's book an interesting insight into this great car from Audi.

Michele Mouton; Grasse, France

Chapter One

FOUR WHEEL DRIVE PREDECESSORS

Most engineers agree that, in principle, it doesn't make a great deal of sense having a car driven by only two of its four wheels. It should thus be underlined from the outset that four-wheel drive is by no means a new development on the motoring and motor sporting scene. It has been toyed with by various designers in various areas of the business ever since the Dutch automotive designer, Jacobus Spyker, produced the first four-wheel drive machine way back in 1902. This ambitiously engineered 8.6-litre six-cylinder car, now on display in a Dutch museum at Uden, produced an early vindication of the four-wheel drive system by being brought to Britain where it won a Birmingham Motor Club hillclimb in 1906, as well as gaining a deal of national publicity when it was driven up the steps of the Crystal Palace Exhibition centre – much to the consternation of the perplexed onlookers.

Despite this early demonstration of the effectiveness of four-wheel drive, such systems did not catch on to any great extent owing to the cost and complexities involved in engineering terms at a time when the big manufacturers were trying to keep down the cost of "motoring for the masses." However, the idea wouldn't go away, and Ettore Bugatti's famous French marque catapulted the concept back into the limelight in 1932 when they constructed a pair of T53 hillclimb specials to contest the prestigious European Mountain Championship events. Powered by 4.8-litre supercharged eight cylinder engines, the Bugatti T53 developed 300 bhp and proved an effective tool in its all to few outings. Ettore Bugatti's son Jean crashed one at Britain's Shelsley Walsh venue during its first season of competition, but while the remains of this machine vanished from the firm's factory after the car building business finally petered out in the mid-1950s, the other T53 survived intact to take a position of pride in the Schlumpf collection museum at Malmerspach.

On the opposite side of the Atlantic, Indianapolis car builder Harry Miller pursued the four-wheel drive trail with a degree of success, and, immediately after the Second World War, the Italian Cisitalia marque commissioned an amazingly complex four-wheel drive machine intended for Grand Prix racing purposes. The Porsche company was commissioned by Cisitalia to complete the design, this elaborate flat-12-engined machine proved to be an expensive white elephant and its only achievement of any note was the setting of an Argentinian land speed record after Cisitalia boss Piero Dusio found himself, in effect, exiled to South America when his business in Italy went bust!

It wasn't, however, until the late 1950s that the four-wheel drive message began to be firmly rammed home by a company capable of translating the concept into a viable commercial reality. Tractor magnate Harry Ferguson had long held the view that four-wheel drive was the way to go, and he helped finance a small specialist company founded by racing driver Tony Rolt and former motor cycle racer Freddy Dixon. In an effort to publicise his four-wheel drive systems, Ferguson Research Ltd was eventually established and embarked on an ambitious programme to develop a four-wheel drive Grand Prix car which stunned everybody in 1961 when Stirling Moss ran away and won the rain-soaked Oulton Park Gold Cup race with it. The Ferguson system was a sophisticated and well thought out four-wheel drive concept, but Ferguson himself had come up against a stone wall of indifference when he tried to interest the British motor industry in the idea of producing a family car equipped with four-wheel drive. The fact that the adoption of such systems would have contributed considerably to road safety (as anyone who has driven a four-wheel drive machine will testify) was lost to the interest of cost-cutting commercial expediency. This lamentable failure to listen to what the Ferguson organisation was preaching is made all the more incomprehensible by the fact that four-wheel drive was accepted as a valid and worthwhile concept when it came to off-road vehicles: witness the success of the Land Rover, Range Rover and other cross-country vehicles such as the Jeep!

Even on the competition side, nobody was interested in the Ferguson Project 99 Formula 1 car, even though Stirling Moss was impressed and convinced of the car's capability, particularly in the wet. Unfortunately, the P99 arrived on the racing scene at a time of relative uncertainty (a new Formula 1 had just been instigated), but when Ferguson offered the project for sale, they were amazed to find not a single team to be interested. It may well have been that the Ferguson system was ahead of its time, for the technical effort applied by BRM four years later – and indeed by McLaren, Lotus, Matra and Cosworth some nine years later – in developing their own, abortive four-wheel drive systems, tends to suggest that they could have made a considerable impact on the 1960s racing scene in those pre-aerofoil days. By the time the Grand Prix teams finally woke up to the possibilities of four-wheel drive, the era of wide tyres and aerodynamic devices had arrived, cancelling out the potential advantages of such an admittedly heavy transmission system.

To this day, Tony Rolt presides over this Coventry-based company, now called FF developments, which specialises in what he describes as "all wheel control", offering a sophisticated four-wheel drive conversion on a variety of machines. The company continues to enjoy a steady business amongst those who are convinced of the benefits affored by such transmission systems, although the individual unit costs remain quite high in the absence of any interest from major manufacturers. Only when the Audi Quattro slipped quietly onto the motoring scene at the start of 1980, did people in the industry wonder "why has it taken so long?"

The Audi Quattro's birth is rooted in modest circumstances. In the mid-1970s, the German Government put out a development contract to both Volkswagen (by then part of Audi NSU Auto Union AG) and Mercedes-Benz, requesting the production of a "jeep-like" off-road vehicles for the German army's use. The Audi combine came up with the Iltis, using a five-cylinder power unit and four-wheel drive, and won the contract in the face of four-wheel drive opposition from what would eventually become known to the public as the Mercedes 'G' wagon. This Iltis was made in many thousands for military purposes and Audi even tried to float a rather more refined version to the public, but its 33,600DM (£9,700) price tag was deemed far too high in 1978 for what was, after all, a rather basic machine with few creature comforts. Nonetheless, the Iltis was to provide the seed corn for the Quattro concept.

Once the Iltis project had been brought to fruition, it became clear to many senior engineers that the development of this efficient four-wheel drive system would have been wasted if there wasn't some further application to which the transmission system could be applied. One of those who advanced this argument most energetically was Walter Treser, a man with a considerable amount of motorsporting background who had rallied and raced at a relatively modest level himself. In March 1977, Treser and his colleagues had installed the Iltis transmission system in a normal Audi 80 saloon and embarked on some preliminary tests in an effort to persuade the Board of Directors that the concept was a viable one. By September 1977 they had made their point and senior test engineer Jorg Bensinger was delighted to inform his team that the four-wheel drive Audi road car project, dubbed A1, had been given the go ahead and allocated the appropriate funding.

In fact, there was a little more to it than that. Walter Treser had acted largely on his own initiative within a company which had strict avenues of protocol, cutting red tape, and in effect, almost presenting the senior management with a *fait accompli*. He had worked on the original four-wheel drive Audi 80 as something of a private "pet project" and the Board's decision to fund it was a cautious one: Treser clearly knew that he would have to produce dramatic results, quickly, if the development's future was not to be prejudiced by those in senior positions who were not convinced.

In 1978 the Audi 80 four-wheel drive development car was sent to Hockenheim where it returned some highly competitive times equipped with a 160bhp engine against its 240bhp rivals. It had been expected that the Audi four-wheel drive system would prove effective on loose surfaces, but this vindication of its performance on tarmac was a tremendously encouraging factor, a portent perhaps of the all-round excellence to be provided by the ultimate Quattro production car. Audi's head of marketing and their sales director were both treated to an amazing demonstration of the prototype's capabilities on Europe's steepest mountain road, the *Turracher Hohe* in Austria, where the car climbed up through the snow on its normal road tyres without any assistance from snow chains.

Finally, came the most spectacular and unconventional demonstration of all. Treser brought a fire engine from the Gaimersheim fire brigade, based close to the company's Research and Development department, and got them to turn their hoses onto a hillside close to the firm's facility. Having thus turned the venue into a quagmire, Treser invited Toni Schmucker, Chairman of the Volkswagen Board, to tackle the hill in a variety of vehicles. Predictably, the Audi 80 four-wheel drive prototype is the only machine that makes it to the top, thus recruiting this key senior personality within the Group to the "pro Quattro" ranks. The development's future was now firmly assured!

The search for an appropriate engine was an interesting story in itself. It was 1975 when Audi decided to launch its new 100 range of saloon cars and it was then that the company's five-cylinder engine was offered as part of a range of three power units, all closely related in their basic design. All three featured cast iron cylinder blocks with integral cast liners and the aluminium cylinder head was fitted with in-line valves operated by an overhead camshaft via bucket tappets. The camshaft was driven by a toothed belt which also drives the jack-shaft on the 1.6 litre four-cylinder unit and the water pump on the 2 litre four-cylinder and 2.2 litre five-cylinder units.

Continuing the Audi trend towards rationalisation of its mechanical components, the five-cylinder engine was closely based on the four-cylinder design, offering the advantage that the two engines have many parts in common and the reliability of those constituent parts had already been proved in the field. With dimensions of 79.5 x 86.4mm, the five-cylinder engine has a longer stroke than the four-cylinder versions in the interests of superior torque characteristics, its great advantage being that it is significantly smoother than the four-cylinder engine whilst not requiring the space within the engine compartment that would be taken up by a straight-six. In a nutshell, it was seen by the Audi engineers as a good compromise cylinder layout and quickly came to be regarded as a power unit of unusual refinement. Careful positioning of balance weights have minimised the vibration problems within the engine/gearbox assembly which were previously regarded as a hindrance in the development of an engine with this cylinder configuration.

Bosch K-Jetronic fuel injection was employed from the outset on Audi's five-cylinder engine, and the unit initially offered a power output of 136 bhp at 5700 rpm. A four-speed gearbox was initially employed, but a five-speed 'overdrive' one was soon made available and the engine was gradually developed with the addition of a turbocharger to the specification which is currently available in the Quattro coupé.

However, the very latest Audi model to be equipped with a version of the turbo five-cylinder engine is the 143 mph Audi 200, which became available on the UK market at the end of June, 1983. This combined a 180 bhp version of the five-cylinder engine with the striking, sleek (0.33 drag coefficient) bodyshell which was first seen on the second generation Audi 100, but incorporating wider tyres and a front spoiler for added stability at high speeds. This blend of power and refined accommodation resulted in acceleration from 0-60 mph in just under eight seconds allied to a touring petrol consumption of near 30 mpg.

With the new Avant aerodynamic hatchback now available, it doesn't take too much imagination to envisage the five-cylinder, 180 bhp turbocharged engine combined with four-wheel-drive from the Quattro, all adding up to a package which would find favour with the sort of people who would otherwise buy a Range Rover – but would really prefer its outstanding qualities packaged in something closer to an everyday road car. Now it's down to Audi to deliver!

It was however back in 1980, at the Geneva Show, that the wraps came off the Audi Quattro. It was unveiled to the public, a square-cut, functional, yet purposefully attractive two door coupé fitted with permanent four-wheel drive, equipped with a 200 bhp turbocharged five cylinder in line engine driving through a splendid five speed gearbox. Initial road impressions left the international press gasping for superlatives. There had been four-wheel drive machines before; there had been high performance coupés before; there had been competition Audis before. But there had never been a package quite like this. Blending impeccable road manners with high levels of adhesion, splendid straight line performance and refined accommodation for four, the Audi Quattro was no "one off" development, no competition special. It was a freely available road machine, built admittedly in relatively modest numbers, but whose success and overall acceptance was due to confound even its most ardent supporters within the Audi organisation. Over the next few years that followed that ecstatic launch in Geneva, the Audi Quattro was destined to revive Audi's image in a manner that had never been done before.

The Audi Quattro was not just going to be a fine road car or an effective rally competition machine. It was going to be the machine which transformed the Audi marque image from that of a rather dowdy, staid producer of sound family saloons, to that of an ambitious, hard-hitting, technologically ambitious car builder. The Audi Quattro became a standard bearer for Audi's new generation, the long-term developments of which are destined to carry the firm's name well on into the 1980s.

Four wheel drive McLaren M9

Four wheel drive Lotus 63 – 1969

Four wheel drive Matra MS84 – 1969

The Audi 100 CD, powered by a fuel injected 136 bhp engine of 2.2 litre capacity with 125 mph top speed and 35 mpg overall fuel consumption. The 1983 car of the year.

*Two possibilities for future four-wheel drive development? The Audi 200 turbo and the
100 Avant CD – only time will tell.*

Chapter Two

COMPETITION WORK

We have seen in the last chapter how Audi's sense of innovation and technical imagination gave rise to the Quattro concept in the first place, but the car's competition development and achievements over the past three seasons amount to a record every bit as impressive as the basic car's impact on the public market. Those early tests at Hockenheim with "hack" 80 saloons equipped with four-wheel drive had not only confirmed the company's thinking that the concept would lead to a fine road car with terrific potential, but they also stirred up long-term thoughts about competition versions of the striking new coupé.

Audi had been involved in saloon car racing and an intermittent programme of international rallies, using the 80 saloon, under the direction of Jurgen Stockmar, although these cars proved to be contenders for class victories rather than outright successes. In fact, at World Championship level the Audi team was not considered to be much of a factor.

However, in the late 1970s there was a ban on four-wheel drive which stemmed from a surprise victory by the AMX Jeep on the US Press on Regardless event way back in 1975. However, a great deal of water had flowed under the motorsporting bridge since that time and the American off-road vehicle's triumph in that rally was beginning to fall into historical perspective, regarded as a one-off fluke success by a number of influential teams. Audi nonetheless had their own firm, and justified opinions about the potential of four-wheel drive and lobbied hard during 1978 for the ban to be lifted. This task involved a campaign of persuasion aimed largely at Renault and Lancia, their respective rallying overlords Gerard Larrousse and Cesare Fiorio eventually acceding to the German marque's requests and "giving the nod" to the Federation Internationale Automobile that they wouldn't oppose such a decision. The feeling at the time was quite clearly to the effect that past experience, both in racing and rallying, indicated that four-wheel drive wasn't a particularly effective solution, and as Audi anyway had not yet proved to be a major force, there was no harm in lifting the ban. Perhaps that was a decision which Lancia and Renault would eventually come to regret…

In September 1979 one particularly interested visitor who called on Audi's Ingolstadt competitions department was none other than Hannu Mikkola. That year he had been briefly involved with Mercedes-Benz and their fleeting return to the rallying stage, while also running some British national events at the wheel of an Escort entered by David Sutton (later to become the entrant of Audi UK's competition Quattros). Mikkola by that time reckoned he had got his plans for 1980 firmed up in his own mind, but at the insistence of Stockmar he felt he had to go and see what Audi had got up its corporate sleeve. To satisfy his curiosity he was given a brief try at the wheel of one of the hard-used "hack" four-wheel drive 80 saloons and expressed himself immediately impressed at the car's high level of traction. Eventually, after a lot of thought and consideration about the project's potential, he agreed to undertake a testing programme with the Quattro during 1980 with a view to a further commitment the following year. At this stage, on the prototype turbocharged Quattro coupé, throttle lag was still something of a problem, as was the tendency to weave around whenever he backed off the throttle. But an awful lot of effort was to be channelled into the project as a whole over the months that followed.

The Audi Quattro was formally homologated into Group 4 on January 1, 1981, the requirement for this international category at the time being a production run of 2000 machines. This was a task easily achieved by Audi who, after all, had envisaged the Quattro as a high performance production car which was to go rallying, unlike Ford's RS1800, Vauxhall's Chevette 2300HSR or the Sunbeam Lotus, all of which were conceived with a specific rallying application in mind but which had to go into a small production run in order to satisfy the Federation Internationale des Sports Automobiles rule requirements.

The competition Quattro had in fact made its public competition debut on Portugal's Algarve rally at the end of October, 1980, where Hannu Mikkola and Arne Hertz were not formally entered but drove as an "unofficial entry" at number zero. Had they in fact been participating, they would have won the rally quite easily: after this performance the Federation Internationales des Sports Automobiles firmly banned such impromptu demonstration runs, but by then Audi's point had been made.

The Group 4 Quattro actually made its rallying debut on the Castrol Janner Rally on January 9-11, 1981. This was the opening round of the European Championship and, since it was run in very snowy conditions, it was no real surprise when Austria's Franz Wittman gave the new car a clear debut win on his home ground.

The Audi factory's World Championship team made its debut with two Quattros in the 1981 Monte Carlo Rally. Walter Treser's continuing influence not only resulted in Mikkola's confirmation as number one driver, but attracted the company a blaze of publicity on all fronts when talented French girl Michele Mouton was nominated as driver of the second car – in the face of a lot of competition from several other established male rivals. Arne Hertz continued to partner Mikkola while Fabrizia Pons took the hot seat alongside Michele Mouton. At that time the rallying version of the 2.2-litre turbos were officially quoted as producing 200bhp, but Mikkola's prophetic words that "the car is amazing on gravel, but not yet fully competitive on tarmac", were to be staggeringly accurate.

There was to be no magical debut victory once the Quattros set out on the highly competitive World Championship trail. Mouton retired from the Monte almost before it had seriously started, contaminated fuel being the reason behind her elimination, while Mikkola built up a six minute advantage in the lead before going off the road permanently. But their performance was good enough to suggest that the German four-wheel drive contenders were on course to upset a lot of established rallying applecarts and it came as no surprise when Mikkola won the car's first World Championship competition success on the Swedish Rally in February, the only true winter rally by then remaining on the Championship calendar.

To this day, however, the Audi Quattro has not really managed to display a significant advantage over its two-wheel drive rivals when it comes to competition on tarmac surfaces. Many theories have been put forward as to why it is still lacking in this area and, certainly, Audi has done a lot of work in sorting out a suitable tarmac suspension set-up for rallying purposes. In the early days they just used the same settings as for the loose, but lowered the whole car by 20mm, but now the latest Group B Quattro has available a lightweight suspension set-up which incorporates many titanium and plastic components. However, even this basically does not do much good for, particularly on the bumpier special stages, the Quattro's problem is that there is not sufficient travel in the suspension system.

Audi in fact spent a considerable amount of time trying to get the tarmac handling sorted out in time for Corsica in May, 1983, where the Group B "evolution" Quattro was due to make its debut. They even recruited veteran Bernard Darniche to try and sort it out, but the five-times Corsica winner managed to badly break his ankle during a testing accident – he hit a privately owned, non-competing Peugeot – but despite these efforts, the Quattros were incomprehensibly blown off by the Lancia Rallys which finished in 1-2-3-4 formation in the event itself.

Stig Blomqvist, who was brought into the team for the first time in the 1982 Swedish Rally – which he promptly won after leader Mikkola ploughed into a snow bank, only for Mouton to arrive and punt him off even further! – reckons that the car's problems on tarmac is with the turbo. The latest evolution model and a limited rev. range with basically nothing below 5500/6000rpm and a maximum of 8000rpm. The current large capacity turbo unit is very difficult to keep on the cam: below 5500rpm you have about 100bhp on tap and when revving the engine in that crucial band between there and 8000rpm, you have up to 420bhp available! On loose surfaces Blomqvist reckons that it is relatively straightforward to keep the turbo spinning by inducing wheel spin, thereby sustaining the revs at a relatively high level. On asphalt, with all that grip from racing tyres, it is very easy for the engine to fall off the cam. Also, on a tight event like Corsica, with all those tight hairpin bends, you don't even have the added advantage of being able to use the handbrake to slide the car round tight turns when you're at the wheel of this four-wheel drive machine!

Although the Quattro originally ran in Group 4 during 1981 and 82, the new Federation Internationale des sports des Automobiles alphabetical groupings came into effect at the start of 1982. However, although the World Championship rally organisers were obliged to run classes for these new categories, there was no corresponding compulsion for the manufacturers to enter them. Lancia, in fact, was the sole front runner to appear with a purpose-built Group B machine, the supercharged 037 Rally, at the start of 1982. But from January 1, 1983, as far as all Federation Internationale des Sports Automobiles approved international championships were concerned, the manufacturers no longer and the choice to stay out. If they wanted to score points in the Championships for Makes and for the Drivers, they were now obliged to field Group B machines. Although both Group 2 and 4 cars were still permitted to take part, neither their manufacturer nor their driver could score points in their respective Championships and, additionally, these cars could not be handled by A or B seeded drivers. That eliminated all the established top drivers who have won major international rallies as well as leading drivers who qualified for nomination on the 'B' list by their national sporting authority.

For Group B, a manufacturer had to build a minimum of 200 cars within a 12 month period. This, at least, was the intent of the regulation. Federation Internationale des Sports Automobiles had announced details of the new Appendix J rules as early as October 1980, and in those early days it was intended that after a manufacturer had built his 200 cars he was then stuck with that particular mechanical specification. The only way the homologation details could be changed was by building a further 200 cars to a different specification and then getting this revised model accepted into Group B all over again. Incidentally, Group A requires a production run of 5000 cars within a 12 month period and the new 80 Quattro model was accepted into this category as from July 1, 1983.

Gradually, however, this stringent stipulation was watered down (a fact which caught Ford out with the abortive 1700T project), and mainly under pressure from certain influential manufacturers, such as Lancia and Talbot, a rule crept in which allowed Group B homologated machines to be followed up by what was called an "evolutionary" version. This, in effect, allowed them to get it right second time round, and although the revised rule doesn't permit a manufacturer to change the entire concept of the car, it is permissible to bring in a lighter, more effective version of which only a further 20 have to be built. Lancia, quick off the mark as ever, were the first to do this with an evolutionary model of the 037...

For Audi it was a matter of re-homologating the old Group 4 Quattro into Group B. The changes were not that drastic, the addition of rounded plastic wing extensions not only enhancing the car's appearance but also contributing to a slight weight saving. However, the car was still left some 40kg away from its Federation Internationale des Sports des Automobiles required 1100kg: weight has always been a problem for the rally Quattro, particularly in Group B guide as the engine was just the wrong size.

Under the Federation International des Sports des Automobiles 1.4-litre turbo equivalency, the 2144cc engine is regarded as a 3002cc normally aspirated engine and the minimum weight regulation is applied accordingly. In order to improve on this situation, the 20-off evolutionary model which made its first appearance in Corsica has a slightly sleeved down engine for 2142cc (2998cc after applying the equivalency) and thus, falling beneath the 3-litre normally aspirated limit, leaves the development team free to work down to a minimum weight limit of 960kg. At the time of writing, they still haven't got down to that figure and are lucky to break the 1000kg barrier!

The evolutionary car had, as standard, some 360bhp available as compared with the quoted 330bhp for the original Group B version. Incidentally, a four-valve per cylinder version has been on the Ingolstadt test beds for some time – destined for the new short wheelbase Quattro, and promises power outputs in the region of 500bhp!

A major change to the specification with the evolutionary car has been the adoption, as standard, of an electronically activated clutch. This was first tried on last year's Royal Automobile Club Rally and they wanted to use it on the 1983 Monte Carlo, but initially Federation Internationale des Sports Automobiles said it wasn't allowable – only to change their minds subsequently. Operated by a button on the gear lever, this system helps the driver to employ a left foot braking technique which is necessary to extract the best from this four-wheel drive machine. It enables the driver to overcome the turbocharger lag, and with the power on at all times, the four-wheel drive system is thus offering its traction advantages for a larger part of the time. The German manufacturer had opted not to employ a "crash" gearbox, such as were employed on the old Mini rally cars, and insist on retaining the regular all-synchromesh gearbox, thus rendering it difficult to carry out clutchless changes in a routine manner without risking a spate of gearbox breakage: changing these units on a Quattro is a long job, of course, taking up to 40 minutes as opposed to the 12/15 minutes on conventional two-wheel drive machines. The electric clutch does however take some getting used to as the pedal itself moves up and down in response to the switch movement: and the kick back from this is reported as being particularly painful if you happen to have your foot in the wrong place at the wrong time!

Compared with other contemporary rally cars, the Audi Quattro is regarded as a labour intensive machine, requiring a considerable amount of attention from specialist mechanics (the Germans have a very individualistic system whereby there are strict demarcation lines) and none of the major components are particularly straightforward to remove and replace. The factory team's servicing record whilst out on events often leaves a good deal to be desired, a reflection perhaps on the company's lack of rallying experience generally and a certain management problem. Team manager Roland Gumpert has been described in the British press as the conductor of an orchestra who also wants to play the main instruments at the same time. He is a man who finds it difficult to stand back and direct the overall scene, wanting to get his hands dirty "under the bonnet" and, in consequence, there has been a tendency for his mechanics not only to rely on him for decisions, but also to sort out specific mechanical problems on the spot.

It took the "evolution" Quattro until August 1983 before it won its first World Championship round, in Argentina (thanks to Hannu Mikkola). It came close to winning both the Acropolis and New Zealand rallies, but both works entries retired with mechanical problems) and, of course, the Lancias trounced it quite convincingly in Corsica. Subsequently Mikkola scored his second win in the "evolution" Quattro when he triumphed on the 1000 lakes, although in this particular event Stig Blomqvist, his team mate, was deliberately ordered to slow down and concede an imminent first place in the interests of Mikkola's drivers' championship aspirations. Prior to this relatively late-season upsurge of success, the Audi board came close to telling the rally team to stop its programme for the rest of the year...or at least until it got itself properly sorted out!

Nonetheless, Audi did triumph in the 1982 Manufacturers' Championship, a fact which is often forgotten within the rallying world. This was certainly a pretty fine achievement in the car's second season of competition, although there is a strong body of opinion which suggests that the Quattro often succeeds despite itself.

Problems aside, the Audi Quattro's impact on the International rally scene over the past three seasons had been considerable. Certainly it has assured the future of the four-wheel drive concept in this area of competitive motorsport: Lancia is currently developing a four-wheel drive variant of the current 037 Rally, Colt are on the verge of unveiling a similar machine and both Ford and BL are obviously interested. Remember, Ford's 1700T Escort rally programme was axed simply because they realised that they had no chance with a powerful rear-wheel drive machine in a four-wheel drive world.

If you have not got four-wheel drive in 1985 on the World Rally Championship scene, then you might as well forget it.

Malcolm Wilson/Mike Greasley on their way to 10th overall in the Quattro used previously by Hannu Mikkola on the Open Championship.

British debut of the Audi 80 Quattro: Harald Demuth/Mike Greasley on the 1982 Mintex, opening round of the Open Championship.

Harald Demuth/Mike Greasley held fourth overall with the 80 Quattro on the 1983 Circuit of Ireland before crashing heavily: although a Gp A specification car, the 80 Quattro was running in Gp B since its homologation into the former category didn't come about for another three months.

Another of Malcolm Wilson/Mike Greasley on their way to 10th overall in the Quattro used previously by Hannu Mikkola on the Open Championship.

Michele Mouton and Fabrizia Pons on their way to second overall on the 1982 RAC Rally with a works Quattro – a good result considering their lack of experience on this event.

Hannu Mikkola and Arne Hertz put in a fantastic performance to win the 1982 Scottish Rally, climbing through the field from last place at the end of the first stage.

Mikkola's Quattro receives attention on the 1982 Circuit of Ireland, an event in which the machine was afflicted by engine bothers.

Michele Mouton and Fabrizia Pons on their way to second place in the 1982 RAC Rally. It was their second attempt at the rally having crashed the previous year.

Stig Blomqvist and Bjorn Cederberg on their way to finishing 1st on the 1983 Scottish Rally.

1983 Open Champions Stig Blomqvist and Bjorn Cederberg win the Welsh Rally in atrocious conditions.

Stig Blomqvist retired from the 1983 Circuit of Ireland when his Quattro's gearbox broke whilst he was leading on the first day.

Stig Blomqvist and Bjorn Cederberg on their way to finishing 1st on the 1983 Scottish Rally.

Engine specialist builder Terry Hoyle works on the engine of Stig Blomqvist's Quattro on the 1983 Scottish where it finished first.

Andrew Cowan/Alan Douglas in an Audi Sport UK 80 Quattro on the 1983 Scottish Rally.

Hannu Mikkola/Arne Hertz in the Audi Sport UK Quattro on the 1982 Manx Rally.

Malcolm Wilson/Mike Greasley on their way to 10th overall in the 1982 Lombard R.A.C. driving the Audi Sport UK Quattro used previously by Hannu Mikkola on the Open Championship. It was the first time Wilson had driven a Quattro on an international rally.

Veteran Andrew Cowan on the 1983 Scottish in a group A Audi 80 Quattro. Cowan was brought in after regular driver, Harald Demuth injured himself in a testing accident. He finished in the top ten co-driven by BBC Scotland's Alan Douglas

Hannu Mikkola/Arne Hertz on their way to winning the 1982 RAC Rally.

Hannu Mikkola on his way to his record fourth win on the Lombard RAC. Co-driver Arne Hertz has won it five times as he won it with Stig Blomqvist in 1971 in a Saab.

1982 Scottish Rally. Hannu Mikkola/Arne Hertz drove from last place to first, snatching win from Jimmy McRae in closing stages. The steering arm had broken on first stage so he had to reverse out!

Enthusiastic Swedes in suitable headgear photograph every angle of the works Quattros entered in the Swedish 1983 rally.

Hannu Mikkola on his way to victory with a regular works Quattro on the 1983 Swedish Rally – note the studded tyres.

UNDERSTEER! Stig Blomqvist's 80 Quattro kicks up the snow on the 1983 Swedish Rally.

Belgium's Marc Duez has had considerable success with his Quattro run by his country's importer. He is seen here on the 1983 Boucles de Spa.

Enthusiastic crowds almost swamp the Audi mechanics as the works Quattros stop at a servicing point in the '83 Swedish.

Getting on with it! Mikkola's Quattro becomes three-wheel drive as he presses on along a bumpy tarmac section on the '83 Monte Carlo Rally.

Michele Mouton's Quattro throws up the spray as it plunges through the ford in Hamsterley Forest during the 1982 RAC Rally.

Business office of a works Quattro, where all the work is done!

Internal and external general views of the Audi competitions department at Ingolstadt, near Munich.

Mouton's Quattro undergoes some quick servicing on the '82 RAC.

Thoughtful – and wet! 1982 Audi crew Harald Demuth (behind wheel) and John Daniels, seen through the screen of their 80 Quattro on the RAC Rally.

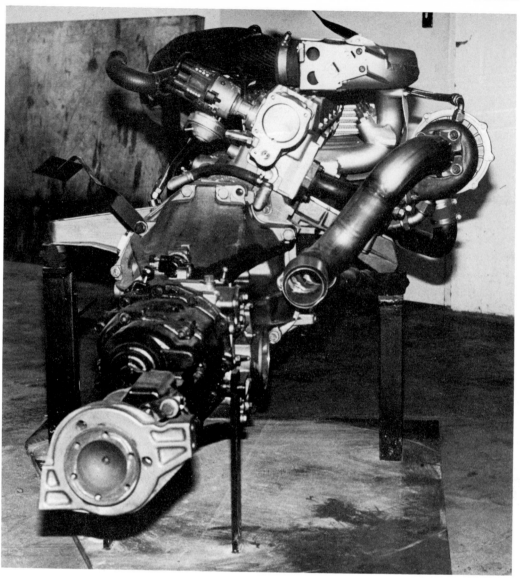

The Quattro engine, installed and out of the rally version.

In its element: an early road test Quattro demonstrates its sure-footed ability in the Swiss snow.

A works rally Quattro bodyshell in the process of preparation at the team's Ingolstadt base.

Watch out the opposition! The Quattro makes its public debut at the 1980 Geneva Motor Show.

Flying high. Michele Mouton on her way to victory in the 1981 San Remo Rally, the first World Championship event to be won by a woman.

Engine of a works Audi 80 Quattro.

The driving seat of the works 80 Quattro.

Michele Mouton's Quattro in action on the 1983 Safari Rally, Kenya.

Spectacular background for Mikkola's Quattro in the 1983 Tour of Corsica. Note the rear wheel off the ground in the second shot.

Mikkola's Quattro arrives at the finish of the 1983 Swedish Rally.

Changing lights on Blomqvist's Quattro, Portugal, 1983.

Stars of the Quattro cockpit, Michele Mouton (left) and Hannu Mikkola.

Mikkola/Hertz scatter the crowds in Portugal, 1983.

The Audi 80 Quattro of Harald Demuth/Mike Greasley being serviced on the 1983 Mintex Rally.

Hannu Mikkola and Arne Hertz, all ready to go!

How photographer Maurice Selden survived, we shall never know! An unusual, yet spectacular, view of Stig Blomqvist's Quattro on the 1983 1000 Lakes.

No-wheel drive! Mikkola aviating to victory on the 1983 1000 Lakes.

Local boy. Vic Preston Jnr's Quattro on the 1983 Safari Rally.

Mikkola looks thoughtful (centre) as the two works Quattros are serviced during the '83 1000 Lakes.

Blomqvist hurtling to victory on the 1983 Ulster Rally, the Quattro's first tarmac victory.

Scrutineering and servicing for the Mouton/Pons and Mikkola/Hertz Quattros on the 1983 Acropolis Rally.

Chapter Three

QUATTRO DEVELOPMENT

When examining and considering the Audi Quattro's evolution and development programme one is immediately struck by two factors. Firstly, the whole project really reached fruition in a remarkably short space of time by motor industry standards and, secondly, how little in the way of complicated development problems bugged the machine's development. Of course, both these aspects reflect just how much of a "technical cocktail" the Quattro really was, relying on an enormous number of established Audi parts and components which could be made ready for use in a short space of time.

After initial consideration has been given to the concept, project engineer Jorg Bensinger anticipated that the end result of his labours would be a straightforward four-wheel drive road saloon that would be capable of taking advantage of any mass-market demand. However Ferdinand Piech, head of Research and Development, decided that if Audi was to take this imaginative technical step forward they needed to exploit it for all they were worth. Audi didn't quite have the cachet of refinement and established technical excellence enjoyed by Mercedes-Benz, and to a lesser extent B.M.W., and since those two established West German car manufacturers and the area of the market occupied by several of their products were within Audi's long-term strategic "firing line", the first four-wheel drive product from Audi had to be truly spectacular. Piech thus agreed that a four-wheel drive project should go ahead, but a high-performance machine should be the number one priority. At the time the current Audi front-wheel drive coupé was in the technical pipeline and it was therefore not a great problem to dovetail the Quattro coupé's development programme with that of the front-wheel drive machine. Although the front-wheel drive coupé was well on schedule at the time the Quattro development was given the green light, the Quattro wound up first on the market.

The Iltis had proved a considerable success for Volkswagen and its sturdy, uncomplicated four-wheel drive transmission system was adapted with little trouble. The Quattro evolved with a five speed manual gearbox, similar to that already proved in service with thousands of five-cylinder Audi 100's, the torque from this unit transmitted to the rear wheels, in addition to the front, via an inter-axle differential and a drive train from the back of the box itself. This design made it possible to adopt components from the Audi 100 and 200 production lines, including the clutch and clutch linkage, the input shaft, gear clusters, front differential, gearbox housing and gearchange mechanism.

The inter-axle differential is integrated in the gearbox, taking up very little in the way of space, and contributing only a very small extra weight penalty. This differential distributes the torque evenly to the front and rear final drives, almost completely compensating for changes in weight distribution caused by variations in throttle application. Audi are quick to make the point that, while it is normally desirable to produce their components to be as light as possible, the mechanical extras necessitated by the adoption of front-wheel drive imposes an unavoidable weight penalty (the inter-axle differential, the propellor shaft, rear differential, rear driveshafts and more complicated rear axle design). However, although the Quattro weighs in at some 75kg more than its equivalent front-wheel drive stablemates, Audi makes the point that the four-wheel drive transmission components weight only about 35kg more than a rear-wheel drive set-up.

Jorg Bensinger considered from the outset that permanent four-wheel drive was the most appropriate configuration for Audi's specialist, high performance road cars. Setting aside the fact that the Iltis project already provided the design team with a tailor-made, established four-wheel drive system, Bensinger explained his preference for a permanent four-wheel drive system thus: "When designing a car, the optimum suspension set-up must be established for one particular drive layout only. A suspension arrangement for four-wheel drive cannot simultaneously give optimum results for front-wheel drive and rear-wheel drive. To relieve the driver of the need to adapt to different transmission arrangements, it's best to have all four wheels permanently driven. Indeed, there is no real reason to incorporate a selector controlling the drive to the second pair of wheels unless the four-wheel drive transmission unit design is not fully adequate for its task."

In designing their four-wheel drive system, Audi avoided the established practice for utility vehicles (such as the Land Rover) whereby a transfer box is added to the enginer/gearbox unit, thus driving the front and rear differentials by means of two propellor shafts running fore and aft. Such a construction takes up a lot of space, is obviously heavy and imposes high frictional power losses which, although perhaps acceptable in a utility vehicle, would not be so welcome in a supposedly high performance road car.

Audi's solution was extremely straightforward and simple, They had already got a perfect front-wheel drive system developed for their road car range, so a logical method would have appeared to be simply continuing the drive directly backwards from the lengthways-installed front-wheel drive transaxle. However, Bensinger pointed out that, particularly in very tight corners, where the front wheels would follow a wider arc than the rear wheels, there would be an unacceptable amount of tyre wear and scrub. If such a system was to be adopted, there would have to be provision for disengaging the drive to the second axle – over which reservations have already been expressed.

Thus the decision was made to integrate the inter-axle differential within the gearbox in a particularly compact manner. The primary shaft, as an extension of the crankshaft, drives the gearbox's output shaft, but this output shaft is actually *hollow*. There is a differential cage at the rear of this output shaft and the gears in this differential drive pinions on the *inner* side of the secondary shaft which transmit the power forward to the front wheels. The propellor shaft simply continues to drive the rear wheels in the normal manner.

Extensive testing has satisfied Audi that a torque distribution of 50 per cent front-to-rear is perfect for this drive configuration with a longitudinally installed engine.

The engine, of course, follows a tried and tested configuration, the turbocharged five-cylinder unit having received considerable acclaim in the 200T saloon. In this connection it should be noted that there is a high degree of interchangeability not only between the Quattro and its fellows within the Audi range, but between all the five cylinder petrol engine variants made by the German company.

The modifications necessitated on the five-cylinder normally aspirated engine in order for it to function with its exhaust driven Kühnle, Kopp and Kausch 26 turbocharger include revised pistons with a bowl-in crown, in order to accomodate the higher compression ratio, as well as a facility to spray cooling oil beneath the piston crown when the oil pressure rises about 35 p.s.i. To cope with the extra heat build-up with the combustion chambers the Quattro's engine is equipped with sodium-filled exhaust valves while revised inlet and exhaust manifolds were also installed. There is a much shorter inlet manifold on the Quattro than on the 200T, the pressure pipe connected to an intercooler mounted behind the front air dam: this intercooler is a major factor behind the extra power developed by the Quattro as compared with the 200T – an increment of 30bhp!

More indication of component standardisation can be revealed from an inspection of the suspension system on the Quattro. McPherson struts are employed all round, the layout at the rear simply being the same as for the front end, merely turned through 180-degrees, along with its subframe, the only difference being that the rear axle transverse links take the place of the track rods. The suspension strut of the Audi 80 and Audi 200 were also adapted for the Quattro, while drive shafts are also "off the shelf" components with two pairs of differing length being used in diagonally opposite positions without any further modification.

The braking system, however, is one area in which the demands of the Quattro's particularly high levels of performance have dictated purpose-built components. Ventilated disc brakes of 280mm diameter are fitted at the front with solid discs at the rear, while the asymmetric power-assisted rack and pinion steering system is also a specially developed addition.

In connection with the braking system it should be mentioned that most enthusiastic drivers who quickly came to appreciate the Quattro's stupendous road performance were quick to enquire precisely how long it would be before Audi introduced a system of anti-locking braking as a optional item of equipment. This anti-locking braking system is highly advanced and has been available for some years on certain other high-technology offerings from manufacturers such as Porsche, Mercedes-Benz and B.M.W. Relying on sensors on each wheel relaying impulses to a central "electronic brain" as to the amount of grip on each individual tyre, the anti-locking braking system allows a very fine degree of "lock-up" control on a conventional two-wheel drive machine. However, when adapting the anti-locking braking system for four-wheel drive cars, it had to be borne in mind that there are no freely rotating wheels as on cars with only one drive axle. Since all four wheels on the Quattro are linked via differentials and the rotating masses of the drive train, the derivation of certain control signals for the operation of the anti-locking braking system proved highly expensive and complicated to develop. Eventually the problems associated with anti-locking braking were solved by means of a new generation of new control electronics and the car was made available with the system in the middle of 1983. However, tests indicated that the anti-locking breaking notwithstanding, it was still possible to lock all four wheels on the Quattro if the front differential lock was engaged and, in consequence, the Quattro's anti-locking braking system was designed to work only when the front differential lock is disengaged by means of the fascia control.

It is generally reccomended to drive without the differential locks engaged in normal conditions found on most tarmac road surfaces, but, while it can be advantageous to engage the centre differential lock for more effective braking on slippery surfaces, it is essential to prevent all four wheels from locking up at high speed.

The Audi Quattro is manufactured on a specially installed specialist assembly line within the firm's Ingolstadt plant, a slow line speed and specially selected personnel guaranteeing an above-average level of quality control on this particular model. This production line had needed more than a passing amount of flexibility over the last two years since it was the original intention only to produce 400 Quattros in order that they could be homologated for competition in the appropriate category. However, it quickly became clear that Audi had underestimated the public's demand for the car. Increasing success in the world of international rallying, allied to the public's perception of the car's merits as a whole, meant that the scheduled volume was progressively increased and now the Quattro has long cast off its mantle as a homologation special and secured a firm place in the company's range of products. Almost 6000 Quattros had been built by the end of 1983 and Audi confidently expect to sell another 1500 models in 1984.

From the point of view of the British market, the Quattro's production volume was a crucial factor when it came to considering whether a right-hand drive conversion should be tackled at Ingolstadt. Clearly, with only an original run of 400 anticipated there was no economic sense behind such a decision, but as the car gradually became more and more sought-after, the British importer (V.A.G., U.K. Ltd.) began to press increasingly for a right-hand drive version and, in response, the factory's Research and Development centre started investigating precisely what would be involved in producing such a car.

In Britain, one small specialist performance equipment company, Richard Lloyd's Silverstone-based GTi Engineering, which had hitherto concentrated on uprating the performance of the high performance version of Volkswagen's Golf models, went into the problem with the idea of producing a limited number of right-hand drive Quattros. This was at the start of 1981, some time before the factory development, and one of the orders for his cars came from Audi's U.K. distributor: specially trimmed inside to a high standard by the Aston-Martin-owned Tickford coachbuilding concern. Although Lloyd admits he got no official response from the German factory, word came back through the Audi grapevine that the conversion was quite acceptable. But with the Quattro production line expanding its output every month, Ingolstadt was obviously keen to satisfy the requirements of its English importer.

In terms of structural work, or the positioning of the engine and power train, conversion to right-hand drive posed no problems. The only real re-vamp involved the positioning of the fluid reservoir for the hydraulic clutch system and there were problems installing optional air conditioning systems. The decision to develop the right-hand drive Quattro was taken at the end of 1981 with the intention of making it available on the United Kingdom market in the middle of 1982: in fact it did not finally make its debut in Britain until the following year.

It is certainly fair to conclude that the Audi Quattro's development and subsequent sales success had the function of a pilot project for the German manufacturer. The success of the project confirmed the original theories behind the validity of the four-wheel drive road car and encouraged Audi to expand the concept into a wider range of road cars. At the time of writing the 80 Quattro remains the sole derivative of the original model but four-wheel drive versions of the 100 are anticipated before long and, anticipated most keenly, a four-wheel drive version of the stylish, aerodynamic Avant station wagon. Fitted with the 200 turbo engine, a four-wheel drive Avant could easily become the flagship of the Audi range, combining go-anywhere versatility with luxury car refinement. A mouth-watering prospect by any standards...

The bottom line to all this technical development is Audi's total conviction that, from a technical point of view, permanent four-wheel drive is the best and safest means of employing high levels of power in a modern passenger car with no problems for the driver in the widest range of differing road conditions. From that it follows that Audi can anticipate four-wheel drive becoming the norm, rather than the exception, for high powered cars, depending on the geographic location and the type of use. In the Audi range, at least, four-wheel drive and front-wheel drive will continue to exist side-by-side as arguably the two best drive configurations – although this is a somewhat sweeping assumption which would be vigorously disputed by rival manufactuers who produce what they would claim to be the rear-wheel drive configurations certainly the equal of four-wheel drive and possibly superior!

The Quattro's development certainly came at a timely moment from the point of view of the marque's world sales. In 1980 Audi's world-wide sales figures were 299,987 units: the following year they were up to 329,246, and in 1982 although they eased back slightly to just over 325,000 cars, Audi produced 193,000 vehicles in the first six months of 1983 and estimate a total of about 400,000 for the entire year. In that time only 6000 Quattros have been built, but their impact on the company's perceived image has been far more significant than their financial contribution to the Audi organisation funds.

Few cars in recent years can have had such a dramatic impact in such a short space of time. Yet there was nothing new about the Quattro in that it didn't break any fresh technical ground in itself. It didn't pioneer four-wheel drive; it didn't pioneer the turbocharged engine; it didn't pioneer successful rally involvement. What it did do was to combine a whole host of desirable mechanical parameters in such a startlingly desirable package that many of its rivals were left wondering why they hadn't done something like it earlier. It wasn't what Audi developed: it was the way in which they executed the Quattro which proved such a sensation.

It has shaken the Audi image, revitalising the marque name in the eyes of discerning and enthusiastic owners throughout the world. The whole concept is an emphatic demonstration of the company's innovative potential. The car's competition activities, with a car closely related to the production version and in a situation which the customer can recognise, have made it abundantly clear that the Quattro is the right concept. It has increased public awareness of the Audi name throughout the world, promoted the capability of the firm's advanced engineering, especially in the areas of handling, weight-saving construction and efficient engine design.

Motorsport is an excellent medium, for all its short-term problems, for a car manufacturer to demonstrate it capabilities. And that greater awareness generated by participation in the sport, the shifting of the marque image towards modern technology and dynamic performance, will enable Audi to continue consolidating sales world-wide at a high level.

And it all goes back to the stumpy little Iltis...

KEY DATES IN THE DEVELOPMENT OF THE AUDI QUATTRO

March 1977 — First appearance of a four-wheel drive Audi – an old Audi 80 is equipped with Iltis components as a mobile test bed.

September 1977 — The four-wheel drive Audi is given a development number – A1 – and development expenditures are authorized.

November 1977 — The first 'A1' is driven and officially logged as a development project.

January 1978 — The 'A1' is presented to management by Audi engineers in a demonstration of the prototype on the Turracher Hohe, Europe's steepest mountain road. In deep snow with gradients up to 23 percent, the car did well – on summer tyres without chains.

April 1978 — On the dry surfaces at the Hockenheim track, the 'A1' with a 160 hp engine turns in lap times very close to other cars tested with up to 240 hp, a key result.

May 1978 — Go-ahead received for completing development of the 'A1' up to production.

Summer 1978 — 'A1' is compared against a variety of other vehicles on a hillside course near Ingolstadt, made into a sea of mud by the local fire department – the 'A1' is the only one to reach the top.

Summer 1979 — A new Audi 80 is used to test the four-wheel drive components, and the 'A1' becomes the 'A2'. This phase of testing included use of a 286 hp engine in the Sahara Desert.

Winter 1979 — A Quattro prototype is tested in its refined form, including the centre differential and concentric driveshaft.

Autumn 1980 — Production of the Quattro begins, at a special assembly area within Audi's Research and Development Centre.

February 1981 — The Quattro becomes a part of Audi's European rally programme, winning the difficult Swedish Rally.

October 1981 — Driven by Finnish rallyist Hannu Mikkola and French co-driver Michele Mouton, Audi Quattro wins world rally championship event at San Remo.

January 1982 — Quattro finishes a close second in the prestigious Monte Carlo Rally.

Spring 1982 — Production of the U.S. model Audi Quattro begins.

Where it all began: the Volkswagen four-wheel drive Iltis.

The flexibility of the Iltis was soon obvious – there was little that it could not tackle

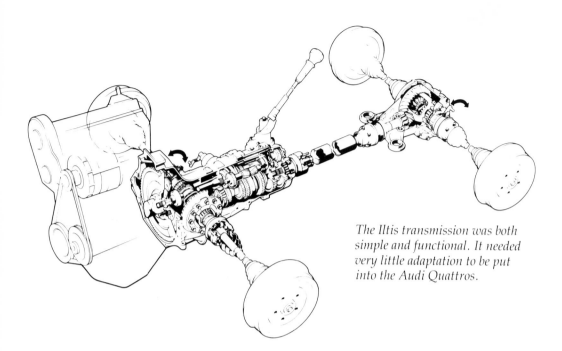

The Iltis transmission was both simple and functional. It needed very little adaptation to be put into the Audi Quattros.

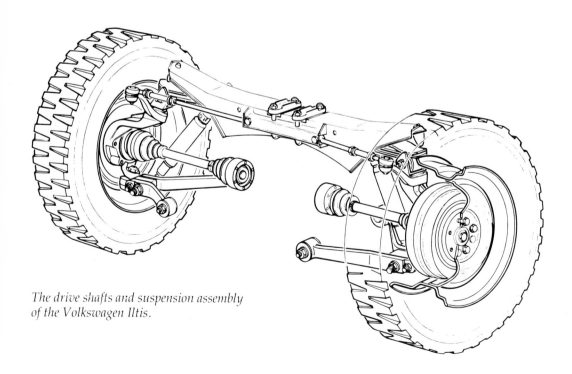

The drive shafts and suspension assembly of the Volkswagen Iltis.

Functional but not pretty! These two pictures show the Iltis both open and closed to the elements.

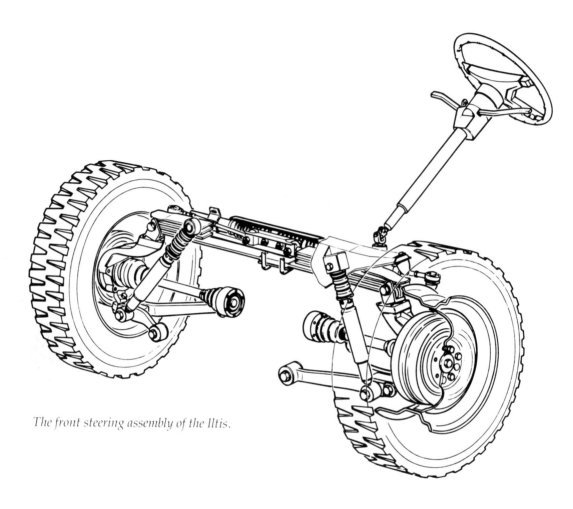

The front steering assembly of the Iltis.

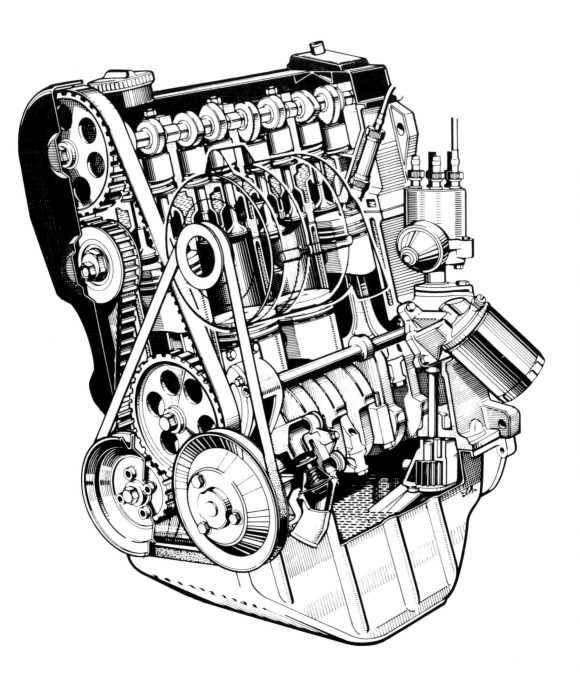

A cutaway drawing of the Iltis' power unit. Robust and sturdy.

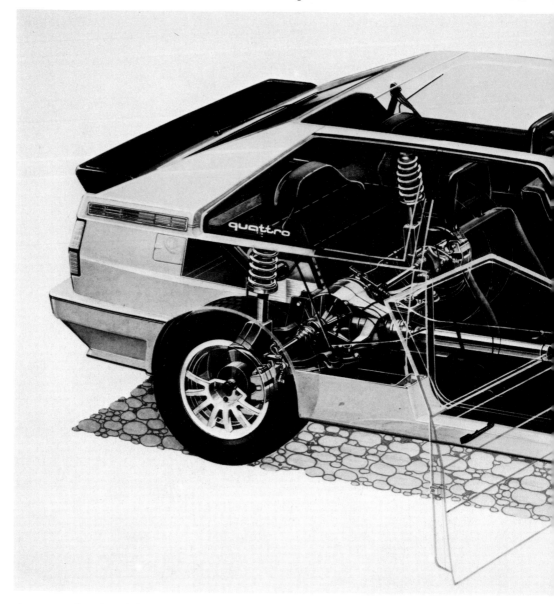

A cutaway drawing of the Audi Quattro Coupé. It shows the mechanical layout in detail and demonstrates what a clever package of mechanics is hidden under the bodyshell.

Chapter Four

MAKING THE AUDI QUATTRO

As has already been mentioned the market success of the Quattro left an interesting production problem to be solved by the Audi management. After all, where does a special high performance coupé with an annual production measured in the lower thousands fit into a manufacturing scheme designed to cope with greater numbers on a daily basis!

The problem certainly did not lie in the advanced technology, indeed, the Audi-NSU group had been dealing with four wheel drive in specialist applications right back to the Munga in the 1950's. Rather it was a matter of fitting the five or maybe twelve vehicles a day into a routine which had been carefully programmed to return a unique level of quality control over a range of fairly standard products.

Not being the kind of people to let multi-million dollar considerations intrude upon a first rate challenge the board decided to meet demand by upgrading the facilities which had been used to build the first homologation run of four hundred vehicles. The actual job of integrating a labour intensive short series run into overall production fell to Dipl. Ing. Balthasar Gültner. By clever compromise and by using highly expensive and ultimately extremely flexible programmable machinery, production became possible by making the necessary body alterations on the main coupé production lines and then feeding the modified bodyshells into the normal body protection and paintwork process.

Perhaps normal is not quite the word to use when describing the Audi paint and protection process. The handling that the body receives can best be equated with the treatment of a special patient in intensive care. Even before the metal is pressed, while still in sheet form it receives its first protective coat. From that point on the tale of the body shell is one of constant cleaning, dipping, phosphorising, neutralising, cataphoretic coating, electrostatic and hand cleaning, underbody priming and PVC coating before the final high gloss paint job.

Its passage through the paint shop completed the body shell travels on its individual trolley to the final assembly shop. Here the real substance of the car comes together. Here the conventions of the super automated factory give pride of place to the ideal of the individual doing his job on an exclusive precision instrument. Even the scale of the building is more reminiscent of a specialist engine builder or race preparation shop than of a part of the massive V.A.G. empire. It is a place which lends itself to a certain *esprit de corps* and the atmosphere reminds one more of a family firm than an international giant.

This atmosphere is no accident. Each worker on the Quattro line has earned his right to be there. In fact one of the greatest problems facing the production engineers at Ingolstadt was the selection of these elite few hundred workers from the four and a half thousand final assembly workers on the main lines.

At Audi it is not customary to speak of line speed when assessing productivity rates. Rather they speak in terms of job cycles, a cycle consisting of the time it takes each worker to fulfill his allotted task on any particular vehicle on the line. On the main production lines these cycles tend to be of one point eight to two minutes duration. The shorter slower Quattro line calls for job cycles of up to, or occasionally exceeding sixteen minutes. Also there is a certain amount of flexibility called for on this line, for instance almost any member of a team would be encouraged to master the job of his work mates as far as possible thus avoiding temporary hold-ups in production due to absenteeism or illness.

Surprisingly this is quite a novel concept in the German automotive industry and one which at first proved difficult to instill into the average line worker at Ingolstadt. Almost any work psychologist or industrial economist has some theory about increasing the intricacy and thereby the interest and the variety of work in factory environments; however all too often they tend to overrate the natural aptitude or even the interest of those whose lot they wish to improve. Thus reasons Herr Gültner and with this in mind he set out from the beginning to make production of the Quattro as prestigious to the line workers as the ownership of the car is to the motoring cognoscenti. When one looks at the overall quality of the end product one must concede that many firms could take a salient lesson in man management from him.

Just how much more complicated the job of the Quattro worker is over his normal production line colleague can in some measure be gathered from the fact, quoted with some relish by Herr Gültner that just to install the voice synthesizer (available now in five languages) involves some twenty six extra wiring operations, each one needing to be done by hand.

Returning to the actual process of assembly, however, one becomes aware once more of the vast resources of the Volkswagen-Audi organisation. From the gear box plant at Kassel comes the transmission and rear drive set up. From the vast Engine foundry at Bad Söden the 2.2 litre five cylinder engine arrives already modified on the production line to take the K.K.K. turbo charger while from the neighbouring machine shops come the modified suspension and brake components.

The fact that the Quattro can stand and in fact revels in fair comparison with any up market sports car in the world speaks volumes for the normal quality of the Audi components. The steering is just one example of cross fertilisation for the steering graces the magnificent 200T and the aerodynamically efficient 100 series cars in exactly the form employed on the production Quattro.

Just how all these components are deployed is also of interest for even to the casual observer it soon becomes apparent that in the Quattro production very little time is lost for men stopping in search of parts. Everything appears ready to hand as if magically thus leaving the men to work their way along the line, each man working his cycle and each series of cycles lasting just one hour on the slow and precise build up of the final vehicle.

At the beginning of the final assembly process each shell sits ready, with its building specification attached, on its individual trolley. Its five coats of superbly applied body protection itself protected in strategic areas by plastic sheeting. One by one as the builders finish each car they will be carefully wheeled through to the final assembly area. Here begins the final evolution in the production process.

Logic is the main governing factor in the final assembly. Door locks must be fitted and then the inner plastic sheeting which protects the door panels and window mechanisms from corrosions. The interior must be prepared to accept the myriad mounting clips for the complicated wiring processes and the first of the anti-drum and sound deadening materials are installed and painstakingly checked before the long process of wiring begins.

The lights and the instrument cluster are the next items to be installed and then very carefully checked. The retaining strips are also made ready to take the glass for the windows and draught proof the doors. Seat brackets and extra wiring must be placed in the car. Each operation of course is done by hand. When these more minor tasks are completed the car is ready for the major components.

The Quattro is now ready for lifting. The suspension components and the front and rear transmisson are already in position for the car on their special stands complete with the engine and even the drive shafts with the brakes ready assembled to drop in. Even as one car is receiving this package another set of components is delivered ready to replace those being used and the stands taken to receive the next but one or two sets.

Forward again and this time it is to allow the fitters access to the top of the engine, everything below having been quickly secured by the engine fitters. This done the car needs only its wheels to be properly aligned along with the lights and the reservoirs for the vital fluids brakes, clutch, radiator etc to be topped up. Door trims seats and any last few unfitted luxuries are added the tank is primed and then the car is taken, complete with trade plates for its first taste of real motoring.

In the course of the final assembly the car can justifiably be said to have had as much individual attention as any well built specialist sports car in the world. Obviously there are a few exceptions, the Aston Martin and the Bristol for example still relying heavily on hand beaten panels which have to be 'shaped' individualy, but if one leaves aside these kind of ultimate luxury carriages the Audi assembly shop must be able to stake a claim to being one of the best 'small' sports car producers in the world.

Even before the car leaves on its test run there are still checks and tests to be run. Nothing is left to chance. The Quattro must carry the flag of V.A.G.

amongst the likes of the BMW 635, the front and rear engined Porsches and even the rather stodgy Mercedes SEC series. In theory it leaves all of them standing and thoroughly vindicates Herr Pieches remark on the cars introduction that it would lead to massive reappraisals among the more traditional sports car manufacturers.

Once through the doors of the final assembly shop the new car turns onto what was once the test track of the old NSU-Audi works which gave the world those marvellous two strokes in the fifties. All being well the driver will cruise slowly around this track, perhaps occasionally stopping if some minor adjustment needs to be made, until the driver reaches the main gates where after presentation of the requisite pass the car leaves to join the traffic. Within minutes the car will be running at full throttle in the conditions for which it was originally shaped. Somehow there can be few better tributes to the engineers and workers at Ingolstadt than a one hundred and fifty mile per hour car fully extended within minutes of leaving the assembly line. Ettore Bugatti, who once told a customer that he need never run in a Molshiem product, would certainly have approved.

Opposite: The first operation as the painted shell reaches the final assembly line commence beneath bonnet with the fixing of sound deadening material, under bonnet wiring, clips etc. Note the sheet of instructions which the fitter keeps within easy distance for constant reference. Beside the line, neatly hung in festoons along the wall so that they fall easily to hand are the leads already sorted into the most efficient order for quick and accurate installation. As can be seen in the lower of the two pictures, the locks have yet to be fitted.

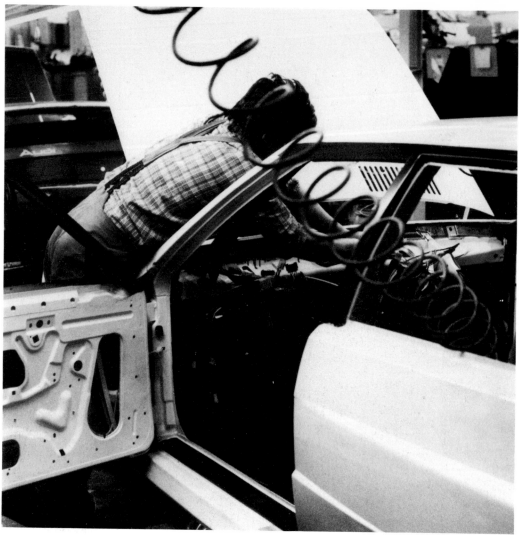

The second stage in the line and the internal wiring is under installation. Most of the leads are already in for the control panel and the lack of any glass in the car is a positive asset in the positioning of the pneumatic equipment used for fixings. The fitter in the picture is taking full advantage of the lack of the windscreen to wire in the heater controls. Before the car moves on it will also have acquired its lights.

Here the sealing strips for the doors and windows are set. The various mechanisms are installed into the doors and the interior lining of PVC sheet is affixed. The instruments are connected and tested and after protective sheeting has been applied to the side of the bodyshell the glass is installed. The car also gathers its exterior mirrors.

With all the ancilliary wiring now installed the car stands realy for inspection. Here the underlay and carpet will be fitted.

At this point the shell is fully wired, tested and inspected. It has also gained most of its interior trim, dashboard mouldings etc. Even the windscreen wipers have been fitted and checked. The boot lining is in and it waits to be lifted for the second phase of final assembly to begin.

Now the bodyshell bids farewell to its individual roller trolley as it is lifted to allow the installation of the pre-assembled engine transmission and suspension units. Again in the background one can see evidence of the efficient storage methods which help to keep time wastage to a minimum. Although none of the skilled workers ever gives the impression of undue haste this line must rank as one of the highest units in terms of man hour productivity anywhere in the automobile industry.

In the fore-ground the ready assembled suspension/engine/transmission units can be seen waiting on their purpose built stands for installation into the next car along while under the raised car a fitter checked the newly installed frontal components. Behind him can be seen the raised platform, just large enough to take both car and crew for the upper engine fixings and electrical connections.

The car has now left the platform and gained its wheels. The brakes are being connected as this picture was taken. Next the tracking will be set and the car will descend once more to ground level.

No car can really be called complete without seats and interior doors panels and at this point those vital ingredients are added.

Now the car can be called complete. The wheel alighnment and balance is checked. The fluid reservoirs are filled. The engine receives its quota of oil and some petrol is added to the tank.

At last the car has moved under its own power. Here finished Quattros await the final inspection before they can be declared assembled.

The final test before the car can be delivered is the half hour or so that the car receives in the hands of one of Ingolstadts test drivers. Inititally he will confine himself to the factory perimeter track until he is satisfied that everything is in order. After this the car is deemed ready for the Autobahn where such is the quality of Audi engineering that the car can be taken up to its maximum speed immediately it reaches its engine operating temperature.

Chapter Five

AUDI QUATTRO – ON THE ROAD

For most sporting motorists, even those with the inclination and funds to purchase some of the more expensive exotica available, the Audi Quattro coupé is a new driving experience. More than that, perhaps, it is a fresh dimension for everyday road motoring, an experience which lives on in one's mind long after they've sampled it and, dare we say, from some specific points of view, makes anything else seem rather lacking.

When the international press first sampled the Quattro in Switzerland at the start of 1980, their reaction was effusive. Journalist after journalist returned to his magazine or newspaper with glowing accounts of how this quite remarkable new German coupé had changed everybody's ideas of what a high performance road car should offer. Inevitably, one would have thought, a certain amount of this unbridled enthusiasm would cool down when they quietly reflected on the car, but that did not turn out to be the case at all. If anything, the legend of the Quattro's road behaviour has grown, rather than diminished, with the passing of time. Three years after it first burst onto the European stage, many people consider that it has no peer.

It initially doesn't strike one as a particularly obtrusive machine. It is squat, square cut and functional in a typically Germanic manner. It lacks the overtly aerodynamic lines of some of its stablemates and its appearance is light years away from the Italianate styling associated with more established "super cars". No, like so many good things, the proof of this Audi pudding is in the eating. On the road is where the Quattro demonstrates its compelling appeal.

Power for the Quattro comes from a five cylinder turbocharged unit which had, prior to the four-wheel drive car's announcement, also been employed in the impressive Audi 200T saloon. Equipped with a intercooler when installed in the two door coupé, the unit developed a healthy 200bhp (DIN) from its 2144c.c. The engine delivers its power in a notably smooth fashion, developing a remarkable 210 lb/ft torque at 3500 rpm. The first indication that the Quattro is really somethings quite special comes when you hold the revs steady at around 4500 rpm. drop the clutch and floor the throttle. Its tyres almost chirping on the verge of wheelspin, the Quattro's combination of acceleration and adhesion pushes its occupants firmly back into their seats as it catapults away. It reaches 60mph in just under seven seconds, quick enough to give Porsche 928 owners something to think about, and it can sprint to 100 mph in just less than 20 seconds. By any objective standards that is quite outstanding: if this Audi coupé was a straightforward front-wheel drive machine, such performance would be regarded as absolutely splendid. But, allied to the high levels of adhesion and security provided by its efficient transmission system, the end result is little short of stunning.

At the other end of the scale, the five-cylinder Audi turbo engine can show off a flexibility and docility which is, quite frankly, almost unnerving. Moments after a sprint through the gears to over 100 mph, it's quite possible to slow right down to 35 mph in fifth gear and then ease the car up through its performance range without even a trace of mechanical shudder or transmission judder. Of course, in these circumstances it takes a little while for the turbocharger to make its presence felt, even when you flatten the throttle, so do not be fooled into thinking that this is an unresponsive machine. Smooth and willing up to 4500 rpm, the engine assumes a more throaty throb above this point from which it rockets round to 6500 rpm with the turbo-charger in full action, an electronic cut-out chiming in at that point to prevent inadvertent over-revving.

There is a reassuring feeling of complete "balance" when you take to the road with a Quattro. The controls are pleasantly smooth and progressive, everything falling perfectly to hand, and this gives a fundamental sense of comfort and well-being behind the wheel. The driving position combines a good relationship between the steering wheel, pedals and gear change with excellent lateral support from the smartly trimmed individual front seats. In most cars many people find a problem achieving the ideal driving position if they're extremely tall: in the Quattro the problem, if anything, faces those below average height. Shorter drivers may find it a little trying that they can only raise the rear end of the seat cushion, paying the penalty for an apparently higher driving position with a lack of support beneath the thighs. However, these are only minor aspects of the car's internal design which do nothing to detract from its fundamental appeal.

The gearchange and clutch are particularly smooth, in typically unobtrusive Audi fashion. You need to depress the clutch quite firmly, and it has quite a long movement, if you're to avoid lightly crunching the gears, but apart from slight difficulty engaging reverse, most people have praised this aspect of the four-wheel drive Audi.

Many people approached the Quattro for the first time wondering inwardly what obvious and/or serious snags would crop up in connection with its four-wheel drive transmission system. Were there any hidden handling idiosyncracies? Any major mechanical gremlins lurking unseen beneath the machine's veneer of newness? Well, the Quattro has now been available on the open market for the best part of three years and nobody seems to have encountered any specific, insuperable problems yet. In fact, to be frank, the whole thing has proved almost a little too good to be true!

In the writer's experience, there have been few things to match one's initial acquaintance with the Quattro. With no perceptible increase in driving effort one suddenly becomes aware that the world has speeded up: the driver suddenly realises that on open, twisting roads, he is catching other high performance cars with incredible ease and no drama. Initially, one can't quite believe the speed at which the car can actually get through corners: one has to "will" oneself to hurl the Quattro through a turn quicker than one's senses feel that it can go. But this is a purely temporary mental barrier. Once successfully negotiated, the sheer driving elation stemming from the Quattro's stability and amazingly high levels of adhesion are simply fantastic. The writer's first encounter with this four-wheel drive car involved regular runs over familiar B-roads with plenty of medium speed, constant radius corners. Corners that, in a 2.8-litre injected Ford Capri or a Saab 900 turbo, could be negotiated with no drama at between 55 and 60 mph. By contrast, the Quattro was rock steady at 70 mph – and one got the firm impression that its ultimate capability was not being approached.

Of course, loss of adhesion at these significantly higher speeds is sometimes fraught with dire consequences, but the Quattro gives more than adequate warning that it is approaching its limits of adhesion. Although pretty well neutral in most circumstances, a touch of understeer at high speed can be taken as a warning that you're probing the outer limits. If you lift off suddenly, there is no sudden lurch to oversteer: the front wheels simply grip again, without causing any dramatic, corresponding response from the rear wheels, and that rock-solid aura of safety and security returns.

As previously stated, McPherson strut suspension is employed all round, the rear end set-up simply being an Audi 80 front suspension unit and subframe, turned around, with the steering arms located by rigid track rods. The end product is a firm, well damped ride, which nonethless insulates the occupants from excessive road noise or drumming through the bodyshell. The car's original specification provided for disc brakes all round complete with vacuum servo assistance, slightly larger ventilated discs fitted to the front as opposed to the non-ventilated ones on the rear wheels. In the vast majority of cases, this braking system has proved fade-free and reliable, quite capable of working in conjunction with the 205/60 VR15 Fulda or Goodyear NCT radial rubber which has been offered as original equipment since the car was first made available to the public.

In wet weather, however, the biggest problem with the Quattro is over-estimating its braking ability. Its traction in wet weather is still virtually beyond reproach, as is its ability to sustain high cornering performance without loss of adhesion. Unfortunately it suffers exactly the same shortcomings as a normal two-wheel drive car when braking from high speed in the wet, and the problems are compounded inevitably by the fact that the other two elements in this equation, its aforementioned traction and cornering ability, means that the Quattro driver is almost always arriving at a point of potential drama significantly quicker than he would be in a two-wheel-drive equivalent. The result tends to be locked up front wheels and earnest concern that the Quattro has yet to be fitted with anti-lock braking: if ever a car needed such an accessory, then it's the Quattro. Elsewhere in this book you will find out why it has taken so long, for various technical reasons, to equip the Quattro with this highly sophisticated anti-lock system which has proved so worthwhile and effective on many other high performance two-wheel-drive cars such as the bigger B.M.W. and Mercedes-Benz saloons. It wasn't finally until the end of 1983, after the Quattro had been available for more than two years, that an anti-braking system was finally provided, the final touch, perhaps to an otherwise almost flawless road machine.

It should be emphasised that, from the outset, the road going Quattro has been produced as a well-trimmed, refined road car with a high level of original equipment, quite in line with anything else in its price bracket (by the end of 1983, the United Kingdom tax paid price was nudging £20,000 for the latest specification right-hand drive version, something of an increase over the original £14,500 demanded for the left-hand drive versions only two years earlier). Standard equipment includes central locking for both doors and the lift-up tailgate, electrically operated windows, tinted glass all round, laminated windscreen, rear window wash/wipe facility, electric heating for the front seats, electrically adjustable door mirrors and a sophisticated radio/stereo system.

There is nothing about the internal appearance of the Quattro's cockpit to mark it aside from any other well-equipped Audi: rocker switches for lights and other ancillary controls are mounted on either side of the main instrument console and vents for the through-flow heating/ventilation systems stretch virtually the full width of the fascia. Each foot well is comfortably wide and there is plenty of space for the largest shoes to operate the clutch, brake and throttle pedals which are well placed in relation to each other for ambitious tasks such as heeling-and-toeing.

Outwardly, the Quattro couldn't be described as extrovert, although the subtly faired, squared off wheel arches tell the tale that this is no two-wheel drive Audi coupé, its less exalted sister model (considerably cheaper) otherwise presenting a near identical profile to the untrained eye. Visibility is quite reasonable from the driving seat in a forward direction, but reversing can be a little difficult, due in part to the high boot line and the rather thick rear pillars. The packaging of the rear differential and drive line equipment means that the boot is necessarily restricted and doesn't have the capacity for more than a couple of soft suitcases. It also holds the inflatable "get you home" spare: there's no way of installing a full-sized spare in the Quattro's luggage compartment.

Straight line stability is notably good with the Quattro, this being one of the by-products of the four-wheel-drive system, but it's worth specifically considering the question of when and how the differential locks should be engaged to make maximum use of the transmission's capability. Generally it is best to drive without the differential locks engaged in normal conditions on dry road surfaces. They can, however, be engaged when the car is on the move, by means of a two-position pneumatically operated control which is governed by a knob in the centre console between the front seats. By pulling out the knob to its first position, the centre differential is locked and in the second position both the centre and rear differentials are locked. This mechanism consists of a dog clutch connecting the differential cage with one output shaft: there may be a slight delay, if the clutch teeth are directly in line, before the lock engages and when they are engaged correctly green indicator lights come on adjacent to the control knob on the fascia.

It can be advantageous to engage the centre differential lock for added confidence on slippery road surfaces, but it's only in conditions of, say, deep snow or heavy mud that this becomes a near necessity. However, it is worth mentioning that if the car is equipped with the optional anti-locking braking system (which became available towards the end of 1983), it should be remembered that, when the differential locks are engaged, the anti-lock system is disengaged. To maintain the high degree of steering control and stability in extreme conditions, it is impossible to use the two systems at the same time. So, when the driver engages the differential lock, the anti-locking braking system switches off automatically and a yellow warning light comes on as a reminder of that fact.

One might expect a car of the Quattro's performance to be a particularly expensive proposition to operate, but the reality is that it is not inordinately costly by the standards of most "super cars". Used with a degree of moderation, it is by no means difficult to squeeze somewhere in the region of 24 to 25 miles out of each gallon of four-star fuel and with a fuel tank capacity of 20 gallons, this translates into a possible range of almost 500 miles, exactly the sort of thing needed for long trans-European trips. Tyre wear doesn't seem to be over dramatic, either, although the front covers clearly wear out rather quicker that those on the rear, bearing in mind that they have to deal with steering loads as well as power, traction and braking. Close experience of this Audi suggests that between 18,000 and 25,000 miles is reasonable, although replacing Goodyear's superb all-weather NCT radials will cost in excess of £500 per set of four.

During the course of its recent history, the Quattro hasn't revealed itself as a car with many hidden bugs or gremlins, but several leading and respected motoring magazines remarked to Audi that they had one or two misgivings about the car's handling when stretched to the limit. As a result, the 1983 Quattros were fitted with modified rear suspension geometry which is intended to keep variations in toe-in to the absolute minimum. These changes have made it possible for the rear anti-roll bar to be dispensed with, while the front anti-roll bar is now mounted on special links for better insulation against vibration.

1983 was also the year in which British buyers at last could obtain a right-hand drive version of the Quattro, a long-overdue arrival which must have disappointed more than a few of the early purchasers who were given the clear impression, when the Quattro was originally launched, that British versions would only be available in right-hand drive form. Indeed, the switch to right-hand drive was pre-empted by one respected British performance tuning company with the result that right-hand drive

Quattros were seen in Britain long before the factory got round to providing one!

There is absolutely no question that the Quattro is currently demonstrating the same levels of mechanical reliability and longevity which characterise the other products of the Volkswagen/Audi combine. It is, on the face of it, a mechanically complex and complicated machine. But because it has been constructed largely from parts which have been proven in other models within the company's range, the Quattro is not only a super car, it is a reliable super car. Those two factors do not often go hand in hand, and the fact that Audi has managed to blend them together in such an appealing, high performance model cocktail is an important feather in the German company's corporate hat.

The simple dashboard and layout of the Audi Quattro. Note the turbo-boost gauge in this left-hand drive version.

Though an out and out sporting car the Audi Quattro is luxuriously appointed inside.

This silhouette shows admirably the sleek lines of the road-going version.

The turbo-charged five cylinder engine on the testbed.

There is not much wasted space when the engine is fitted to the car.

The view that most other motorist see!

From the front the flaired wheel arches and front air-dam are clear distinguishing marks of the Audi Quattro.

At home in the hills. Here four-wheel drive adds enormously to the pleasure of fast driving.

From every angle the Audi Quattro shows it rally breeding.

The snow of course is the Audi Quattro's element – the essential après-ski accessory for the eighties!

Masses of torque and firm traction make the car ideal for towing even if speed restrictions make it a frustrating experience.

Off-road work doesn't have to be dramatic – simply useful at times.

Fiercer looking Quattros have visited Monte Carlo while rallying but elegance is the key note in the road-going version.

Ideal transport for the succesful vintner!

The driving position allows the five-speed gearbox and the differential locks to fall easily to hand. The controls are clear, uncluttered and confortable.

The squat appearance of the Audi Quattro deceives. This coupé is a genuine four-seater.

Servicing is not a job for the amateur. Note that the radiator is completely set-off to the driver's left while the space on the right is given over to the turbocharger.

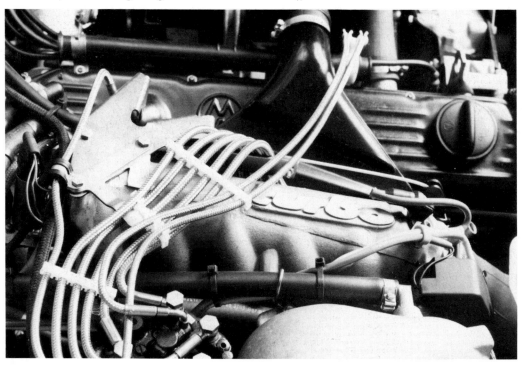

An unsual view from beneath the front and rear differentials.

Chapter Six

THE AUDI 80 QUATTRO

In a way, the pattern of the 80 Quattro's development has been the reverse of what one might logically have expected. So frequently in the past, a manufacturer has produced a basic model in a particular range and then followed it up with specialist high performance variants. In the case of the Quattro and its derivatives, the opposite had been the case. From the initially anticipated limited production run of the Quattro turbocharged coupé, Audi quickly realised that the scope of a four-wheel drive high volume mahcine was significantly wider than they had originally anticipated. Thus, three years after the original Quattro's launch, the four door saloon 80 Quattro made its debut on the European market, a much more modestly equipped machine which enabled Audi's highly efficient four-wheel drive principle to be extended to a wider buying public.

Launched with an initial production run of only 33 cars per week, it didn't take long for Audi's Ingolstadt factory to expand output to more than 300 units per week and, by the time the car became available on the U.K. market in June, 1983, a total of 6500 Audi 80 Quattros had been produced. The recipe was straightforward and simple. Take the compact, yet roomy, 80 saloon – a tried and proven design of which some 30,000 have been sold in Britain alone since the car's debut in front-wheel drive form in 1979, and package the Quattro four-wheel drive transmission system into it.

The 80 Quattro's floorplan is actually taken from the Quattro coupé, along with the gearbox, rear sub-frame, suspension rear springs, rear differential, propellor shaft and road wheels. Like the coupé, the 80 Quattro's suspension is independent on all four wheels, but the front suspension is altered with the incorporation of lighter struts, different springs and dampers. The same speed-sensitive power steering is also utilised from the Quattro coupé and gives the expected well-balanced blend between ease of use and adequate feel.

Unlike the Quattro coupé, however, the four door 80 saloon version employs a non-turbocharged version of the 2144cc, five cylinder fuel-injected engine, developing 136bhp. This engine is also employed in the front-wheel drive Audi coupé, an attractive high-volume, machine which uses virtually the same bodyshell as the Quattro coupé, but the addition of a three-branch exhaust manifold gives the saloon a slight power advantage of 6bhp over the front-wheel drive coupé. Of course, with its more complex four-wheel drive transmission system the 80 Quattro is much heavier than the front-wheel coupé, the additional transmission components accounting for an extra 75kg and the larger four-door bodywork the remaining 65kg.

The 80 Quattro demonstrated its big brother's secure road manners, free from any dramatic vices, and imparts the same safe and supremely secure feeling of high adhesion and stability. Endowed with its less powerful engine, of course, the 80 Quattro feels as though it could never lose its grip on the road in any circumstances whatsoever. The adoption of the Bosch K-Jetronic injected 5-cylinder engine gives the car a relaxed appeal, with plenty of torque and flexibility to compliment its pure performance. It's obviously not in the same league as the turbo Quattro, but the 80 Quattro nonethless has a top speed of just over 120 mph which, allied to a 0-60 mph acceleration capability of 9.2 seconds, makes its performance pretty respectable by the standards of most four door family saloons.

The 80 Quattro's five speed gearbox combines four relatively close ratios with a high "overdrive" fifth, all controlled by a very positive change with a short lever movement. More so than on the Quattro coupé, the steering on the saloon seems just a touch over-sensitive, but once a driver has got used to this, and the steering gains extra feeling while its power assistance diminishes at higher cruising speeds, the whole demeanour of the car is taut and finely balanced.

As regards interior trim and general level of appointment, the 80 Quattro isn't so lavishly equipped as the Quattro coupé, and the basic surroundings feel a little austere even though they are leavened by the incorporation of such refinements as electrically operated front windows, sports seats, central locking and interior adjustable twin door mirrors. The car's 15 gallon fuel tank provides the 80 Quattro with a range of 400 miles-plus, a factor that will appeal to many potential customers as this saloon returns almost 30 mpg during the course of normal day-to-day use.

To the untrained eye, the 80 Quattro betrays little outward indication that it is anything out of the ordinary. But history may just judge it to be a far more significant machine than the more glamorous Quattro coupé with its dramatically higher performance. The 80 Quattro can be regarded as something of a marketing breakthrough, a car which offers the mechanical sophistication of four-wheel drive at a relatively modest price. Through economies of scale, Audi have produced a technically imaginative machine for general sale which is not exorbitantly expensive, one which underlines the benefit of the four-wheel drive system as a widely available feature of an everyday car.

The unaggressive look is deceptive. The Audi 80 Quattro with a fuel-injected five-cylinder engine will travel at 120mph and this comes together with four-door, four-wheel drive practicality.

Chapter Seven

THE QUATTRO SPORT

Possibly the most exciting focal point of attention at the 1983 Frankfurt Motor Show, the Audi Quattro Sport is undoubtedly the most striking and dramatic version of the German coupé yet to emerge. With a power output of 300bhp, a distinctively shorter wheelbase and a top speed of almost 160mph, the Quattro Sport will form the basis of all future works rally entries as well as offering private owners a potentially fully competitive machine as well. The rally machines, with their dry-sump engines with new four-valve cylinder heads, will boost the power output to around 450bhp at 7500rpm, quite sufficient to sustain the Quattro Sport at the very forefront of international rallying.

By shortening the wheelbase of the production Quattro by about 12.6in (320mm), the four-wheel drive coupé becomes very much more a two-plus-two machine rather than a full four seater. But will become an even more nimble and agile rally contender as a result of this major chassis revision and extensive use of Kevlar fibre panels means that the Quattro Sport will be as light as possible without losing anything in terms of structural integrity.

The car's braking system comes directly from the rally programme, incorporating four pot calipers all round with 26mm thick ventilated steel discs. The anti-lock braking system is available on the Audi Quattro Sport road versions as well as being provided on the planned rally versions of the car.

The Quattro Sport's engine development programme has been carried out under the direction of former Alpina engineer Dr Fritz Indra. Audi sees the power unit as a "fourth generation" turbocharged unit and an aluminium alloy cylinder block is employed, partly to compensate for the additional weight for the four valve head and the significantly larger intercooler required to deal with the additional power output. Already fully tested in pre-production trials, the rally-derived block is 23kg lighter than the previously employed cast iron five-cylinder unit: the block's construction follows a new manufacturing technique, the aluminium alloy being cast directly round thin walled cast iron cylinder liners.

The four valves per-cylinder arrangement has enabled Audi to produce a cross-flow cylinder head for the five-cylinder engine. The two camshafts are closely spaced so that the intake cam can be driven from the exhaust cam directly by means of a pair of helical gears running inside the head. A double-flow induction system, rally specification intercooler, revised cast exhaust manifold and a highly sophisticated electronically controlled injection and ignition system completes the mechanical package of this dramatic looking Quattro variant.

The brutally effective and aggressive lines of the short-wheelbase Audi Quattro Sport are well shown off in these three shots.

Chapter Eight

THE TRESER QUATTRO

At the opposite end of the scale to the 80 Quattro saloon, the Quattro coupé hasn't taken long to catch the attention of the specialist customising market which has thrived over the past few years producing tailor-made "bespoke" variations on mouth-watering production saloons from marques such as B.M.W. and Mercedes-Benz. As far as the Quattro is concerned, when former Audi rally team manager Walter Treser established a specialist preparation company in Germany it was obvious that any development programme he might focus around the Quattro would be well worth examining. And so it has proved, this distinctively re-worked coupé variant now capable of sprinting to just over 140mph whilst shaving a few tenths of its 0-60 acceleration times as well as demonstrating a great deal of increase in mid-range performance.

Modifications available to customers for the Treser Quattro include uprating the turbocharged five-cylinder engine to produce an extra 50bhp, revising and lowering the suspension set-up, fitting Bilstein gas filled shock absorbers, adding special Michelin TRX tyres on alloy road wheels which incorporate vane-styled cooling ducts plus a host of apparently cosmetic body alterations which endow the Quattro with a distinctively different profile. In the interests of added stability and aerodynamic efficiency, a deep-skirted front spoiler is added in addition to a fresh rear valance and a distinctively upswept tail section. The British importers for the Treser range of performance parts emphasise, however, that any combination of these performance/aerodynamic alterations can be fitted to a customer's existing Quattro without the complete package, which costs more than £7000, having to be purchased at one specific time.

The engine modifications include larger valves, revised fuel injection, polished exhaust and inlet ports, different high-lift camshaft and an up-rated turbocharged unit delivering slightly more boost pressure than the regular Kühnle, Kopp and Kausch unit with its standard wastegate arrangement. Although the performance increments don't look particularly outstanding on paper when considering acceleration from rest, the Treser Quattro failing, for example, to register any improvement on the standard car's 0-70mph time of 8.3 sec. However, acceleration in fourth and fifth between 80 and 110mph is significantly improved and although the ride is a touch firmer than the standard car, the high levels of adhesion and stability remain impressively consistent.

To purchase one of the Treser Quattros, brand new, in England would cost in the region of £26,000. That's an enormous amount of money that takes the potential buyer well into Porsche and Ferrari territory: but it's a tasteful conversion based on a highly desirable, high technology starting point. A tempting alternative without any doubt!

Walter Treser's development on the Quattro theme incorporates dramatic body styling as well as more power under the bonnet.

Chapter Nine

THE QUATTRO TRIUMPH IN THE R.A.C. LOMBARD RALLY

It was tough, well quite tough. It always is. And although this year the mild autumn weather made the 1983 R.A.C. Lombard Rally neither the hardest nor the most memorable of Britain's biggest motor sport occasions, a deserved victory was earned by a fine British car in the form of the Audi Sport U.K. Quattro and a superb quick driver, Swede Stig Blomqvist, the British Open Champion.

It was a sweet win for Blomqvist, who has been playing the second string driver in the Audi team to the odds-on favourite Hannu Mikkola, aiming for a third R.A.C. win in succession with his four wheel drive Audi Quattro. He failed in his hat-trick despite a brilliant drive that at one point saw him work his way up from twenty-sixth to second place. But a crash on the Sunday never allowed the 41-year-old Finn a realistic glimpse of victory. He fought to second for the third time in his career, 9 minutes 53 seconds behind the Swede. There was little compensation for him in the fact he had won the race four times before.

But the dominance of the Scandinavian squabble between the sharply-hewed Audis did not completely overshadow the glamour of Britain's finest rally, a brutal five day country spin that is an ultimate test for both man and machine.

To celebrate ten years of sponsorship by Lombard the R.A.C. altered the format of the 1983 event by starting a day earlier, including more competitive mileage than before and incorporating town centres as locations for controls and service halts.

There were seven sections that led the drivers from Bath through the grounds of stately homes in the Midlands and on to the forests of Yorkshire, Northumberland and Scotland. The cars then flicked back to the Lake District, a right turn across North Wales, down to Swansea and then on to Bath.

It is one of the longest and toughest events in the World Championships with a route of five hundred miles of special stages with forty of those miles over asphalt roads. It is also the only round of the World Rally Championship which does not allow drivers and co-drivers to recce the route before the start. As far as the drivers are concerned the R.A.C. is seen as a real test of their bravery and reactions, coping through the different, twisting forests in all conditions. And this year, with one of the best entries seen all season, was no different.

It was at Longleat, a country home for relocated wild animals, that the lions of motor rallying including the Audis first began to roar. The five-mile lap that took the cars around the big cats' enclosure gave the Scandinavians a flying start and showed to every other competitor that it was the Quattros that the rest of the world was going to have to beat.

Even a wayward lead to Blomqvists injection box, that lost the Audi a little of its power, only cost a few seconds and left him just behind Mikkola. In the first of the fifty-nine stages the Audis had shown their mud flaps to a strong Toyota team, with three Celica Turbos, and Ari Vatanen in his Opel who was frustrated by sticking brakes. It was not to be his rally. He later retired with a blown gasket.

On the Saturday night the cars clattered back to the city for an overnight halt before shooting up a variety of motorways at crack of dawn for the start of the competition proper that evening.

Already there had been one casualty with the Audis. Pretty Michele Mouton had had some 20 litres of water tipped into her petrol tank and that made her less than pleased. The other Audi drivers, both from the German team and the David Sutton Audi U.K. effort, seemed troubled with engine problems, mostly minor.

The Sunday Spectator stages took a toll of some of the top cars, including Vatanen's gasket. Nissan lost their only works car when Tino Salonen crashed. The Opel hope of Marc Duez failed when he retired his Manta GTE with camshaft failure.

But it was Mikkola's row with a log that was the most tragic casualty of the day. He only finished his stage after a delicate boot-balancing act by co-driver Arne Hertz. And it was clear after that that the Finn had lost any real chance of a third consecutive victory.

On a cold, clear Sunday night the contestants took on the forests in the forty-mile Dalby test. It was a difficult, muddy time in the longest test of the event that was successfully fought by Blomqvist who overtook Henri Toivonen's Opel three quarters of the way through.

But it was the forest Slaley that was to really hammer the top drivers. Three of the top ten including Toivonen, Juan Kankkunen in his Toyota and Antero Laine in his Audi shot over the first firebreak. Spectators helped all three and they managed to continue with little damage.

A short while later John Buffum, who had pushed his B.F. Goodrich-shod Quattro into the top ten, rolled it onto the roof.

Out of the chaos of Slaley came the order. Blomqvist was followed by Bjorn Waldegaard in his two litre, twin-cam turbo Toyota, Mikkola and Jimmy McRae, Britain's only A-seeded driver in the event, in his Manta 400.

And it was how the order was to remain on through Monday until the Scottish border forests. There the treacherous black ice added immeasurable difficulties as the muddied machines tore through the trees. By Carlisle Waldegaard had lost his second place to Mikkola and McRae with a puncture lost his position to a tenacious Russell Brookes in his Vauxhall Chevette HSR.

When the cars returned to England Waldegaard got in further difficulties when he lost a wheel in Grisedale and Toivonen retired in the same forest when his car blew a head gasket. Meanwhile the Audis ploughed on, their commanding lead more firmly entrenched after Grisedale.

A sunny dawn broke on Tuesday after the drivers had spent the night in the magnificent Lake District town of Windermere. Blomqvist emerged from his hotel firmly in control with the rally beginning to look as if it belonged to him and Audi Quattro. And to underline he was in control he took twenty-five seconds off Hannu Mikkola. The competition up front was over and both men understood that fact as they headed south to Liverpool and then to Wales for the final 200 miles of stages.

Behind them the first forest of that day was depressing for McRae who had a puncture and dropped his place. And it was so punishing for Kalle Grundel in his Volkswagen that after he collected his time from the marshals promptly drove straight into a car parked just after the control.

By Tuesday night there was no question which team was in command. The Quattros filled half the top ten, until Antero Laine exited from the competition when his Audi caught fire.

Freezing temperatures left no one in any doubt about the problems that were going to be had on the last night. As Jimmy McRae explained, 'The Audis are running ahead so they are polishing the surface and we are left to skate around. It's all a bit exciting.'

It was quite a compliment to the Audis. On the final stages through Wales and onto Bath the Quattros had a virtual monopoly of the race. It was Jimmy McRae who broke the monopoly by driving brilliantly to finish third in his Opel Manta. He had never finished higher than eleventh before. He was five minutes clear of Lampi in his Audi although twenty minutes behind the leader.

Stig Blomqvist was grinning from ear to ear as he rounded the car park in Bath knowing that he had beaten the best of them. His Quattro, built in Germany and looked after by the Audi Sports U.K. mechanics had behaved impeccably well. And he had been delighted with the Pirelli NT tyres which he had used exclusively throughout the rally. 'Very happy...Thank you,' he said after the finish unable to shake the smile from his face.

It was bitterly disappointing for Hannu who once again missed out on his hat-trick. But he managed a brave smile, 'To be either first or second on this rally for the last seven years is not so bad', he said. 'And this time it was very special because I have seen parts of Britain I never knew existed before. And I will remember Kielder for a long time. Usually it is rain and snow but this time it was nice to be able to see where we were going.' After

McRae came Lampi in his Audi, then Russell Brookes in the Chevette with John Buffum sixth in his Quattro.

It had taken 11,400 marshals, 286, timekeepers, 212 doctors, 78 control officials, 59 stage commanders, 11 regional organisers, five stewards and Stig Blomqvist to demonstrate the magnificence of the Audis.

For it was the cars triumph as much as the men who drove it. The R.A.C. rally is a brutal test for a machine. Reliability is as important as speed and the four Audis in the top six proved that there are few cars in the rallying world at the moment that can hold a candle to them.

There were three Audi Quattros among the leading retirements. Michele Mouton was out at the seventeenth stage after an accident, Antero Laine retired at the forty-first stage because of fire. Only at the fifty-second stage when Darryl Weidner was forced to retire with turbo failure did a Quattro fail to finish because of a mechanical problem.

Audi deservedly took the team prize for the rally which has as much esteem as either the Monte Carlo or Safari rallies. Lancia had already secured the 1983 Manufacturers Championship and did not enter the rally.

It was Audi Quattro's third successive win in Britain's premier rally, five days of hard fast rallying that proved that Audi is a World Championship car despite losing the title this year to Lancia.

Chapter Ten

THE QUATTRO IN THE U.S.A.

The problems besetting any European manufacturer selling in the United States can be adequately summed up in just four words: Federal Environmental Protection Agency. The complex task of cleaning up the emissions, bringing lights and fender heights into line and installing the mandatory impact absorbant hardwear front and rear tends to reduce the marketing and engineering departments to a state of near collapse.

Even though most European countries call for crash tests which are at least as thorough as those demanded by the Federal authorities these often have to be done yet again for the complete satisfaction of the U.S. standard setters. Not only are the Federal standards highly stringent but certain states with specially awkward problems, for instance the ever present peril of smog in California, enforce even more rigorous targets of efficiency upon the would be importer.

Bearing all these factors in mind and also realising that the Quattro was originally a homologation special, it ranks therefore as a minor triumph of marketing over accounting that the Quattro was launched into the U.S. market at all. However introduced it was and it can justifiably be said that the gamble of introducing the Quattro has paid both financial and public relations dividends with a higher percentage of overall production departing to the States with each passing month.

When introduced to the waiting press the car immediately became a cult with the type of exclusive set who would normally be seen at the wheels of the higher denomination number of Mercedes Benz or Ferrari coupés. The reasons for this acceptance are obvious when the loss of performance of such up market exotica are considered. Here for the U.S. enthusiast was a genuine one hundred and forty miles an hour plus machine with a zero to fifty time of just 5.3 seconds and a Federal Environmental Protection Agency quoted consumption of some twenty eight miles per gallon on the highway and a reasonable seventeen miles per gallon in town use.

To further enhance the cars acceptance level with this select fraternity all those extras which the Europeans had been specifying as 'options' were included in the on-the-road basic price. Thus to complement the already luxurious interior such niceties as power windows, electrically adjustable heated mirrors, automatic central door locking, air conditioning, stereo radio and cassette, sunroof, heated seats and rear wiper were included in the package – for the Americans as well as the European buyers.

Useful non-standard options were confined to lockable differentials and pleated leather trim for the interior.

The alloy wheels of the European car were featured as were the low profile radial tyres, the paintwork was to the same high specification and so was the cloth interior. In his original press release Porsche-Audi PR supremo Fred Heyler made a lot of good use of the four-wheel-drive road car which needed no more than five or so inches ground clearance of the standard production saloon. He also emphasised the overall commitment to safety which had gone into the original planning of the car all under the head of 'AUDI'S EXOTIC QUATTRO – THE ALL WHEEL DRIVE GT CAR.'

Another facet of the car which Porsche-Audi's U.S. marketing people in Michigan siezed upon to highlight the novelty of design was the remarkable low efficiency loss in the Quattro all wheel drive system, some three per cent being quoted, compared to the more traditional drives then current in the U.S. market.

So successful was the Quattro in the U.S. that it was merely a formality tht the company would follow it with the U.S. version of the Audi 80 Quattro under its American nomenclature of the 4000S. Released to the U.S. population on the thirtieth of November 1983 Porsche-Audi claimed a genuine 115 bhp giving a genuine top speed of 115 mph again quoting the Environmental Protection Agency for fuel consumption of twenty one miles per gallon around town and twenty eight out on the highway.

With the launch of the 4000S Quattro the press department had stopped referring to even three per cent efficiency loss in the drive train happily claiming, 'the Audi all-wheel drive system is at least as fuel efficient as any two-wheel-drive system'. Much was made also of the new electronically controlled KE injection system whch had allowed the car to meet the emission regulations with such a small loss in power. Parallels were also drawn between the chassis layout of the 4000S Quattro and its larger and more exclusive brother the Quattro.

Once more the specification was extremely comprehensive with all the equipment of the larger car included in the basic price. Options were listed as only metallic paint and a two way sunroof. The release closed with resounding words, 'Priced at $16,500, the affordable Quattro is sold and serviced by a nationwide network of over 400 Audi and Porsche dealers through the U.S. Like all Audis the 4000S is covered by a new two-year limited warranty which carried no mileage restriction'. A statement of confidence which can only bode well for the future.

Front and rear (overleaf) views of the American specification Audi Quattro. The cars are distributed in the U.S.A. by the Porsche Audi Company based in Troy, Michigan.

AUDI 80 QUATTRO – TECHNICAL DATA

Engine:	Five cylinder in line, cast iron block and light alloy cylinder head. Valve gear driven by toothed belt. Single overhead camshaft and bucket tappets. Mechanical fuel injection with air jacketed injectors. No turbocharger.
Bore and stroke:	79.5 x 86.4mm
Capacity:	2144cc
Maximum power:	136bhp at 5900rpm
Maximum torque:	130 lb/ft at 4500rpm
Transmission:	Five speed gearbox, four wheel drive permanently engaged. Three differentials with those between the front and rear axles, and between two rear wheels, lockable by means of control on fascia. Gear ratios: 1st, 3.6:1; 2nd, 2.125:1; 3rd, 1.458:1; 4th, 10.71:1; 5th, 0.829:1; Reverse, 3.5:1. Final drive, front and rear, 4.111:1.
Brakes:	Twin circuit braking with discs all round, ventilated on front wheels, solid on rear wheels. Vacuum brake servo and pressure-sensitive brake regulating valve.
Suspension:	Independent front and rear incorporating coil springs and lower triangular wishbones.
Fuel capacity:	15.2 gallons.
Wheels:	Steel 5½J x 14
Tyres:	Steel radial 175/70 HR14
Kerb weight:	2623lbs
Wheelbase:	8ft 3in
Track:	55.2in (front)/55.4in (rear)
Turning circle:	34ft 5in
Length:	14ft 4½in
Height:	4ft 6.2in
Width:	5ft 6.2in

AUDI QUATTRO – TECHNICAL DATA

Engine: Five cylinder in line, cast iron block and light alloy cylinder head. Valve gear driven by toothed belt. Single overhead camshaft and bucket tappets. Electronically controlled fuel injection system. Exhaust driven KK turbocharger with intercooler. Six bearing crankshaft, electronically controlled ignition.

Bore and stroke: 79.5 x 86.4mm

Capacity: 2144cc

Maximum power: 200bhp at 5500rpm

Maximum torque: 210 lb/ft at 3500rpm

Transmission: Five speed gearbox, four wheel drive permanently engaged. Three differentials with those between the front and rear axles, and between two rear wheels, lockable by means of control on fascia. Gear ratios: 1st, 3.6:1; 2nd, 2.125:1; 3rd, 1.360:1; 4th, 0.967:1; 5th, 0.778:1; Reverse, 3.5:1. Final drive, front and rear, 4.889:1.

Brakes: Twin circuit braking system with discs all round, ventilated on front wheels, solid on rear wheels. Hydraulic brake servo and pressure-sensitive brake regulating valve. ABS anti-lock system

Suspension: Independent front and rear incorporating coil springs and lower triangular wishbones.

Fuel capacity: 20 gallons.

Wheels: Light alloy 6J x 15

Tyres: Steel radial 205/60 VR15

Kerb weight: 2844lbs

Wheelbase: 99.3 in

Track: 55.9in (front)/57.4in (rear)

Turning circle: 37ft

Length: 14ft 5.4in

Height: 4ft 4.9in

Width: 5ft 7.8in

AUDI QUATTRO SPORT – TECHNICAL DATA

Engine:
Five cylinder in line, all aluminium alloy block and cylinder head. Four valves per cylinder, twin overhead camshaft: inlet cam driven directly from exhaust cam by pair of helical gears. Electronically controlled fuel injection system. Exhaust driven KK turbo charger with intercooler. Six bearing crankshaft. Electronically controlled ignition.

Bore and stroke:
79.3 x 86.4mm

Capacity:
2133cc

Maximum power:
220bhp at 6500rpm

Maximum torque:
282 lb/ft at 4500rpm

Transmission:
Five speed gearbox, four wheel drive permanently engaged. Three differentials with those between the front and rear axles, and between two rear wheels, lockable by means of control in cockpit. Gear ratios: 1st, 3.5:1; 2nd, 2.083:1; 3rd, 1.368:1; 4th, 0.962:1; 5th, 0.759:1; Reverse, 3.455:1. Final drive, front and rear, 3.875:1.

Brakes:
Twin circuit braking with ventilated discs all round. Hydraulic servo and pressure-sensitive regulating valve

Suspension:
Independent front and rear incorporating coil springs and lower triangular wishbones.

Fuel capacity:
20 gallons.

Wheels:
Light alloy 9J x 15

Tyres:
Steel radial 225/50 VR15

Kerb weight:
Not officially quoted

Wheelbase:
88in

Track:
58in (front)/57.4in (rear)

Turning circle:
37ft

Length:
13ft 7in

Height:
4ft 4.9in

Width:
5ft 10in